AF252086

GABRIEL GATÉ'S *indulgences*

GABRIEL GATÉ'S *indulgences*

photography by john hay

A Sue Hines Book
ALLEN & UNWIN

First published in 1999
A Sue Hines Book
Allen & Unwin Pty Ltd
9 Atchison Street
St Leonards, NSW 1590, Australia
Phone: (61 2) 8425 0100
Fax: (61 2) 9906 2218
E-mail: frontdesk@allen-unwin.com.au
Web: http://www.allen-unwin.com.au

National Library of Australia
Cataloguing-in-Publication entry:

Gaté, Gabriel, 1955– .
Gabriel Gaté's indulgences.
Includes index.
ISBN 1 86508 079 9.
1. Cookery. I. Title.
641.5

Compiling editor: Angie Burns Gaté
Designed by Ruth Grüner
Photography by John Hay
Food styling by Fiona Hammond
Typeset by J&M Typesetting
Printed in Hong Kong by South China Printing Co.

1 3 5 7 9 10 8 6 4 2

Photography credits
The publisher would like to thank:
Earl Carter and *Vogue Entertaining & Travel* for the photographs on pages viii, x and 16;
Andrew Lehmann and *Vogue Entertaining & Travel* for the photograph on page 101;
George Seper and *Vogue Entertaining & Travel* for the photographs on pages 36 and 74;
Simon Kenny and *Vogue Living* for the photograph on pages 48–49;
Chris Chen and *Vogue Entertaining & Travel* for the photograph on page 142;
John Hay for the photographs on pages 11, 137 and 172;
Simon Griffiths for the photographs on pages 24, 40, 61, 85, 92, 116, 124, 148 and 162;
Mark Chew for the photograph on page 96;
and Gabriel Gaté for the photographs on pages 28, 30, 38, 53, 98, 115 and 121.

To André, my brother the baker

acknowledgements

Gabriel Gaté's Indulgences is the result of much cooking, travelling, eating and dreaming. It was a team effort. Many thanks to Angie, my wife, who took part in almost all aspects of the project.

Thanks to Sue Hines and Allen & Unwin for making the book possible, and to John Hay, Fiona Hammond, Ruth Grüner, Sarah Dawson, Foong Ling Kong and to all who contributed to the production, marketing, publicity and distribution.

I am grateful for the help of my two sons, Sebastian and Michael, and to many friends, especially Mario's greengrocer's shop in Toorak, in particular Terry Greguol, Peter Bourchier butcher shop in Toorak, all at Claringbold's fish shop in the Prahran Market and John Cester Poultry at the Prahran Market.

I would also like to thank French Style, Supply & Demand, The Conran Shop and Hospitality Dinnerware for their generous loan of props, and Jeremy Strode, Virginia Dowzer and Max Dowzer Strode for their kind photographic permission.

contents

introduction

We all need to enter a fantasy world from time to time. So, to escape the humdrum of our daily lives, we dream of love, of having time to enjoy good books and fine music, of freedom and of holidays. And we dream of being pampered with delicious food.

I will be satisfied if this book makes you dream, but its real aim is to help you make at least some of your dreams come true. In it you will find a collection of recipes for all occasions: many of the dishes are quick, while others may take a little longer. But they are all easy to prepare and they are all in some way, to me at least, an indulgence, perhaps for their delectable ingredients, for their seasonality, or for the ambience they create. I became a *cuisinier* for the simple reason that I love to indulge myself with simple, beautiful food. For me, indulgence rhymes with beauty, exotica, quality, finesse and freshness, rather than with excess. A freshly caught fish barbecued with fine herbs and shared with loved ones in a relaxed setting— this, for me, is a great indulgence. So it is not just the food, it is also the place, the occasion.

You will find many words in this book about ingredients and about shopping for them. To be a happy cook, you need to discover the pleasures associated with preparing food and to take the time to make food shopping fun. Get to know the shopkeepers from whom you buy: you can learn much and they will serve you well.

To be a happy cook, you also need to learn to relax and enjoy it. Take advantage of the prepared foods that now abound in delis and markets, and don't try to do too much yourself. At the same time it can be enormously satisfying to cook new dishes. Variety is truly the spice of life, so the more you increase your repertoire the happier cook you'll be.

Best wishes and happy cooking.

breakfasts
and brunches

There is something about a lazy weekend breakfast that appeals to everyone and makes us feel pampered. At Chez les Gaté we occasionally treat ourselves to a special breakfast, perhaps out in the garden if it is a sunny morning. We start with freshly made juice, using our prized electric juicer to create exotic blends such as orange with pineapple and pear or with mango and passionfruit. Our choice of fruits depends on what's in season. As well we toast our favourite breads, or perhaps buy croissants from the local French *pâtisserie* and serve them with raspberry and apricot jams. The aroma of freshly brewed coffee hangs in the air, the mood is relaxed and *la vie est belle*.

We find leisurely weekend brunches a great way of catching up with family and friends. Breakfast can then drift into lunch, and the food can be a bit more elaborate: you might serve some good cheese, cold meats and antipasto, or use free-range eggs to cook a herb omelette, scrambled eggs or eggs en cocotte. For the recipes that follow, preparation time is usually minimal. If you wish you can make your fruit juice in advance: if so, just add a little sugar and cover the container before refrigerating it overnight.

Good food, a glass of champagne and then perhaps a lively game of pétanque or cricket. What a perfect way to pass the morning.

gruyère and chive soufflé

SERVES 6

50 g (about 2 oz) butter, plus a little extra for greasing the moulds

50 g (about 2 oz) plain flour, plus a little extra for dusting the moulds

500 ml (2 cups) cold full-cream milk

3 egg yolks

120 g (about 4 oz) gruyère cheese, grated

salt

a pinch of cayenne

¼ tsp grated nutmeg

a pinch of cream of tartar

6 egg whites

3 tbsp finely snipped chives

It is easier to make a successful savoury soufflé than a sweet one, because the white sauce holds everything together. For extra substance, add a cup of diced cooked vegetables, perhaps asparagus, leeks or capsicum, to the white sauce before you fold in the egg whites.

Preheat the oven to 200°C/400°F. Butter and flour 6 individual soufflé moulds.

Melt the butter in a medium-sized saucepan over a medium heat. Whisk in the flour and cook for 3 minutes without browning. Slowly whisk in the cold milk until the mixture is smooth, and cook over a low heat for 4 minutes. Remove from heat and mix in the egg yolks and cheese. Transfer to a large mixing bowl and season with salt, cayenne and nutmeg.

Add a pinch of cream of tartar to the egg whites and beat them into stiff peaks. Mix a little of the egg-white mixture into the cheese sauce and add the chives. Gently fold in the remaining whites, using a rubber spatula or large spoon. Fill the moulds, flattening the tops and wiping off any mixture from the rims of the moulds.

Place the moulds on an oven tray and cook in the preheated oven for about 15 minutes. The soufflés should rise at least 2 cm (1 in) above the rim of the moulds and the sides should look dry. If you're unsure whether they are cooked, leave them in the oven for an extra 2–5 minutes. Place the soufflé dishes on plates and carry them carefully to the table.

masala omelette

SERVES 2

1 large tomato

½ small green chilli

½ small onion, diced

4 large eggs

salt and freshly ground black pepper

1 tbsp vegetable oil

1 tbsp fresh coriander leaves

I learned to make this popular Indian dish while visiting a spice plantation in the Kerala region of southern India. There, top hotel chefs execute it in minutes at the breakfast buffet table.

Halve tomato, then squeeze out and discard the seeds. Dice the flesh.

Remove the seeds from the chilli and cut the flesh into thin slices.

Break the eggs into a bowl and beat with a fork for about 10 seconds, until just mixed. Season with salt and pepper.

Heat the oil in a non-stick pan over a high heat, add the onion and stir for 1 minute. Add the chilli and diced tomato, stir for 10 seconds and then stir in the coriander. Add the eggs, stirring so they cook rapidly, until the egg is set. Cut the omelette in half and serve immediately.

spicy breakfast compote

SERVES 2–3

2 medium-sized quinces

1 tbsp caster sugar

6 dried apricots

6 prunes

¼ vanilla bean, halved

a 3 cm (1½ in) cinnamon stick

4 coriander seeds

3 black peppercorns

½ tbsp orange zest

1 tsp lemon zest

When quinces are not in season, you can use pears, nashis, plums or nectarines. At breakfast I prefer this dish cold. But it also makes a delicious dessert served hot with ice-cream or rich cream.

Peel, quarter and core the quinces. Place in a saucepan and cover with water. Add the remaining ingredients, bring to the boil and simmer for 20–25 minutes or until the quince is tender.

If you are serving it cold, allow the fruit to cool in the liquid and then chill it in the fridge. For a hot dessert, transfer the fruit to a bowl and boil the liquid down by half. Reheat the fruits in this liquid before serving.

french eggs en cocotte

SERVES 2

20 g (about ⅔ oz) butter

2 tbsp Italian-style tomato sauce

2 tsp grated parmesan (optional)

4 eggs

salt and freshly ground black pepper

One of my favourite breakfasts. Cooked in a small soufflé mould, an egg en cocotte reminds me of my childhood in France. Adapt the dish to your taste by replacing the tomato sauce and parmesan with ham, smoked salmon, cooked mushrooms or fresh herbs.

Preheat oven to 200°C/400°F.

Butter four individual soufflé moulds. Place ½ tablespoon of the tomato sauce and ½ teaspoon of the parmesan in the bottom of each mould. Break in an egg, season with salt and pepper, and top with a small knob of butter.

Place moulds in a small oven tray. Pour about 2 cm (1 in) of boiling water into the tray around the moulds. Cook in the preheated oven until the egg whites are set but the yolks are still soft, which will take about 10 minutes. Serve immediately, with toasted country-style bread.

tortilla with chorizo and asparagus

If you are catering for a large group, make several small tortillas rather than one large one. In this recipe I use chorizo (a Spanish salami-style sausage), mushrooms and asparagus. But feel free to create your own version.

SERVES 2

8 asparagus tips, about 6 cm (2 1/2 in) long

1 tbsp olive oil

1/4 brown onion, thinly sliced

4 medium-sized oyster mushrooms, halved

1/2 clove garlic, finely chopped

4 eggs

salt and freshly ground black pepper

60 g (about 2 oz) chorizo, finely sliced

Drop the asparagus into a small saucepan of boiling water. After 1 minute, drain and put aside.

Heat half the oil in a non-stick frying pan, about 25 cm (10 in) in diameter. In it cook the onion slices over a medium heat for 2 minutes. Add the mushrooms and garlic, and cook for another 2 minutes.

Break the eggs into a bowl and season with salt and pepper. Add the cooked onion and mushrooms, the chorizo and the asparagus.

Heat the remaining oil in the same pan (no need to wash it). Add the egg mixture and cook over a medium heat without stirring. When the under side is cooked and the top has started to set, place a plate over the pan and turn the omelette out onto it. Return to the pan, uncooked side down, and finish cooking for 1–2 minutes.

Serve the tortilla hot or cold. You can cut it into wedges and serve it as a snack or nibble.

sangria (a spanish punch)

Serves 10

1 orange

1 lemon

1/3 cup cognac, brandy or Grand Marnier

2 tbsp caster sugar

a bottle of good red wine, chilled

500 ml (2 cups) freshly squeezed orange juice

400 g (about 14 oz) strawberries

2 bananas

2 kiwifruit

2 pears or apples

My version of this popular Spanish drink has a moderate alcohol content, so that everyone can safely enjoy two glasses.
If possible, make it several hours in advance to let the fruits impart their flavour to the liquid.

Wash the orange and lemon. Cut off the ends, slice the fruits thinly and then cut the slices in half. Place in a bowl with the cognac and sugar, and refrigerate for several hours.

Add the chilled wine and the orange juice to the orange and lemon slices. Wash, hull and slice the strawberries and add them too. Peel the bananas, kiwifruit and pears, and cut them into small pieces. Add all the fruit to the punch bowl and chill for at least 30 minutes before serving.

mango, orange and pear juice

Serves 2

1 ripe mango

2 oranges

3 ripe pears

Select just-ripe pears and mangoes for this richly textured juice. If you must, make the juice in advance but add a little sugar and then cover and refrigerate it.

Peel the mango and cut into small pieces. Peel and segment the oranges. Peel, quarter and core the pears, then cut the quarters into 2 lengthwise.

Feed the fruit through the juicer and serve immediately.

scrambled eggs with truffle

Truffles have an extraordinary intensity of flavour. This is one of the best ways to experience their fragrance—just warmed through, in creamy scrambled eggs.

SERVES 2

1 small fresh truffle, 20 g (about 2/3 oz)

4 large eggs

salt and freshly ground black pepper

30 g (about 1 oz) butter

2 large slices of wholemeal or country-style bread, toasted

If possible, store the eggs (in their shells) and the truffle in a covered container in the refrigerator overnight: the porous shells will allow the eggs to absorb the truffle fragrance.

If the truffle is dirty, brush it briefly under cold running water. Slice thinly, then cut into match sticks. Break the eggs into a mixing bowl and beat with a whisk until runny. Add the sliced truffle, keeping a few pieces for garnish, and season with salt and pepper.

Melt half the butter in a small pan over a very low heat. When just melted, add the eggs and cook slowly, stirring all around the bottom and sides of the pan to prevent sticking. The eggs must remain smooth and creamy.

Toast and butter the bread when the eggs are almost cooked. Whisk the remaining butter into the eggs and spoon them onto toast. Serve immediately.

pineapple, pawpaw and orange juice

SERVES 4–6

1 medium-sized ripe pineapple

1 medium-sized ripe pawpaw

4 oranges

A very satisfying mixture of tropical flavours with a lovely texture. A glass first thing in the morning will put a smile on your face!

Peel, quarter and core the pineapple, then cut the flesh into small pieces.

Halve the pawpaw and remove the seeds. Peel pawpaw and cut the flesh into small pieces.

Peel and segment oranges.

Feed the fruit through a juicer and serve immediately.

If you must keep it for a few hours, stir in 2 teaspoons of caster sugar, cover with plastic wrap and refrigerate until required.

spiced potato pancakes
with coriander

Aromatic and an ideal weekend dish, either on its own or with grilled fish, meat or poultry. You can vary the flavour by using other herbs and spices.

MAKES 4 PANCAKES

500 g (about 1 lb) potatoes
salt and freshly ground black pepper
about 2 tbsp vegetable oil
½ medium-sized brown onion, finely chopped
1 tsp curry powder
2 tbsp finely chopped fresh coriander
1 tbsp chopped parsley
20 g (about ⅔ oz) butter

Peel and grate the potatoes. Season with salt and pepper, and place in a strainer.

Heat a tablespoon of the oil in a small non-stick pan and stir-fry the onion for 3 minutes without letting it brown too much. Stir in the curry powder, mix well and transfer to a bowl. Squeeze the grated potatoes in your hands to remove the excess moisture. Combine the potatoes with the onion, coriander and parsley.

Heat the butter and a little of the remaining oil in a non-stick pan over a medium heat. Place a quarter of the potato mixture in the pan and use a spoon to flatten it into a thin pancake. Cook for 3 minutes, then turn the pancake over and continue to cook until the second side is done (about another 3 minutes). If you find turning the pancake difficult, slide it out onto a sheet of baking paper and then return it to the pan uncooked side down.

Cook the other pancakes in the same way, adding a little oil to the pan if necessary. Keep the cooked pancakes in an oven at 100°C/210°F, but avoid overlapping them. If you must stack them, place baking paper in between.

THE BAKER

The warm fragrance of freshly baked breads and croissants, the artful display of loaves of all shapes and sizes, and trays of irresistible cakes and delicate pastries make visiting a modern bakery a great pleasure. All over the world there has been a renaissance among bakeries, with new technologies and techniques improving the look, variety and flavour of bought breads. Many bakers make their bread in full view of the customers and many contemporary bakeries double as a café where we can sit and enjoy the atmosphere and the gastronomic delights on offer.

I love bread and at weekends I buy a couple of loaves of different texture and flavour to complement particular foods. We like olive, herb or capsicum bread for brunches and barbecues, or with an antipasto selection. With a fresh seafood platter I usually go for a rye bread, and for sandwiches a light sourdough is perfect. And with French food, what else would you want but a baguette?

A good bakery offers more than you may at first think. Several of my favourite bakers sell uncooked puff pastry, which saves me a lot of time when I need some for a special meal. Not all bakers provide this service, but if you are polite and friendly the chances are they will. Occasionally I also buy uncooked bread dough for pizzas and foccaccias … Bakers—what would we do without them?

GOOD YEAR
BMW
BOSCH
ROUYSSALET
PNEUS
S.A.
Belle des Champs
TEL : 91.49.54
j'ai
la carte
de vie
DUNLOP SP 55 M+S
90
PNEUS CRAMPONNÉS
RED EX

ham and parmesan risotto

Close your eyes and savour each grain of this classic dish. The saltiness of the ham enlivens every mouthful.

SERVES 3

1 tbsp olive oil or butter

½ onion, finely chopped

3 cups chicken stock (page 165)

1 cup arborio rice (Italian round-grain rice)

150 g (about 5 oz) finely shredded ham

3 tbsp finely grated parmesan

2 tbsp chopped parsley

salt and freshly ground black pepper

Heat the oil or butter in a medium-sized non-stick saucepan and gently fry the onion for about 2 minutes. In a separate pan, bring the chicken stock to a simmer.

Add the rice to the onion and mix well. Add about a cupful of the stock to the rice and bring to a gentle simmer, stirring occasionally with a wooden spoon. Simmer until almost all the stock has been absorbed, then add another cupful. Continue in this way, adding stock a little at a time until the rice is cooked but still slightly firm in the centre. (If you run out of stock, add a little boiling water.) The rice takes a total of about 20 minutes to cook: when it is ready (the risotto should be creamy, not runny), add the ham, parmesan and parsley. Season to taste with salt and pepper, then turn off the heat and cover the pan. Leave to rest for about 3 minutes before serving.

olive and sundried tomato focaccia

MAKES 16–24 WEDGES

1 quantity of focaccia dough (page 171)

2 cloves garlic, very finely chopped

3 tbsp extra-virgin olive oil

4 tsp finely chopped fresh oregano or 2 tsp dried oregano

1 tsp sweet paprika

a pinch of ground chilli

freshly ground black pepper

24 Greek olives, pitted and halved

24 sundried tomatoes, halved

2 tsp sea salt

3 tbsp finely grated parmesan

No one can resist the warm yeasty aroma of focaccia just out of the oven. Make sure you have enough, as it will disappear like hot cakes.

Once you have formed the dough into two balls, leave it to rest for 10 minutes.

Preheat the oven to 250°C/500°F. In a bowl mix the garlic, olive oil, oregano, paprika, chilli and some black pepper.

Roll out or press the dough into a circle or oval 1.5 cm (¾ in) thick. Rub or brush this with the olive-oil mixture. Press the olives and sundried tomatoes deep into the dough and sprinkle with a little sea salt and parmesan. Bake in the preheated oven for about 10 minutes, or until the base is cooked and lightly browned underneath.

mushroom and fontina pizza

1 quantity of pizza dough (page 171)

400 g (about 14 oz) mixed mushrooms

4 tbsp olive oil

2 shallots or 1/2 brown onion, finely chopped

3 cloves garlic, finely chopped

1/2 tbsp finely chopped fresh oregano or
1 tsp dried oregano

salt and freshly ground black pepper

1 cup Italian-style tomato sauce

300 g (about 11 oz) fontina cheese, grated

3 tbsp finely chopped parsley

16 black olives, pitted and halved

Fontina is a lovely Italian cheese with a nutty taste and a texture not unlike that of gruyère. It melts beautifully, making it delicious on gourmet pizzas like this one. Treat yourself and buy some exotic mushrooms, wild ones if available.

Form the dough into two balls and leave to rest for 10 minutes. Trim the mushrooms, then wash and slice them. Heat half the olive oil in a large frying pan over a high heat and sauté the shallots and mushrooms for a few minutes until soft. Remove, drain and leave to cool.

Preheat the oven to 250°C/500°F. Roll the dough into rounds about 1 cm (1/2 in) thick or less. (You can stretch dough by pulling it gently.) Place these bases on greased oven trays.

In a small bowl mix the remaining oil, half the garlic and the oregano. Season with a little pepper and brush the pizza dough with this seasoned oil. Spread a little tomato sauce on top and sprinkle with a third of the cheese.

Season the mushrooms with a little salt, pepper, parsley and the remaining garlic, then spread this over the pizzas. Sprinkle with the remaining cheese and press in the olive halves. Bake in the preheated oven for 15–20 minutes or until the bases are cooked and lightly browned underneath.

grilled eggplant and tomato pizzas

MAKES 2 PIZZAS, EACH
SERVING 2, OR MAKES
16 WEDGES

1 quantity of pizza dough (page 171)

2 medium-sized eggplants

6 tbsp olive oil

salt and freshly ground black pepper

8 medium tomatoes, about 5 cm (2 in)
in diameter

3 cloves garlic

1 cup fresh basil leaves

1 cup Italian-style tomato sauce

300 g (about 11 oz) grated mozzarella

16 black olives, pitted and halved (optional)

The aromas are irresistible. You can adapt this version to your taste by using other vegetables such as zucchini and capsicum.

Shape the dough into two even balls and set aside for 10 minutes. Wash the eggplants and slice into rounds about 1 cm (½ in) thick. Brush with a little olive oil and cook on a hot grill or in a non-stick frying pan until soft. Transfer to a plate and season with salt and pepper.

Preheat the oven to 250°C/500°F. Halve the tomatoes. Blend the remaining oil (there should be at least 4 tablespoons), the garlic and the basil leaves into a purée and season with salt and pepper.

Roll pizza dough into two rounds or one large rectangle, about 1 cm (½ in) thick or less. (You can stretch the dough by pulling it gently or pressing it down.) Place the bases on greased oven trays and brush with some oil. Brush the cut side of the tomatoes and one side of the eggplants with the purée.

Spread the pizza bases with the tomato sauce and sprinkle with about one-third of the mozzarella. Top with the eggplant slices and tomato halves (cut side up). Sprinkle with the remaining cheese and press in the olive halves.

Bake the pizzas in the preheated oven for 15–20 minutes or until the bases are cooked and lightly browned underneath.

lunches
and barbecues

A tangy radicchio salad served with marinated and barbecued chicken fillets, accompanied by a lightly chilled chardonnay or rosé and followed by a fruity dessert or delicious cake. Whether we are lunching indoors or outside, I like to keep the cooking simple, with few last-minute preparations required. It was a tradition during my youth to make lunchtime something of a celebration. My father would often praise the virtues of eating well in the middle of the day, rather than at night. Certainly it is true that the cook is less tired and everyone feels more leisurely. And, of course, any excess in which we indulge while so relaxed can be comfortably digested before bedtime.

Barbecues are a popular way of entertaining informally, especially during the day. And no wonder: there is something about cooking out in the fresh air that makes it easy to relax. It's a great way to spend a few hours, and as a bonus there are no saucepans to wash afterwards!

Barbecue equipment is now quite sophisticated and may include hot plates, an oven arrangement, roasting spits and even wok burners. Whatever apparatus you have, there are a few common rules to remember when barbecuing. Always preheat the barbecue well before you cook: turn all the burners on until the cooking surface is hot, then reduce the heat or switch off part of the barbecue according to the quantity you have to cook. It is wise to keep one side of the barbecue hotter: start cooking here, then transfer to the cooler side any food which is almost ready or has started to burn. Don't cook directly over the flame and never allow the food to burn, for burnt food is carcinogenic. Lastly, to make things easier next time round, clean the barbecue before it cools down.

mediterranean mussel soup

with saffron

800 g (about 1^3/$_4$ lb) mussels

^{1}/$_3$ cup dry white wine

freshly ground black pepper

1 tbsp olive oil

1 tbsp butter

^{1}/$_2$ small leek, finely sliced

1 small carrot, finely sliced

^{1}/$_4$ small fennel bulb, finely sliced

2 pinches of saffron threads

400 g (about 14 oz) canned peeled tomatoes, finely chopped

1 small potato, sliced

salt

a 100 g (about 3^1/$_2$ oz) fillet of white fish, e.g. flathead or snapper

a pinch of cayenne

2 tbsp cream

1 clove garlic, finely chopped

2 tbsp finely snipped chives

A fine light meal when accompanied by toasted bread which you have brushed with some olive oil and chopped garlic. In the south of France, we would drink a Rosé de Provence with it.

Wash the mussels well in a large amount of cold water, rubbing the shells vigorously against one another to remove the grit. Place in a large saucepan with the wine and a little black pepper. Bring to the boil, cover the pan and cook for a few minutes until the shells have opened. Shake the pan once or twice during cooking time, to allow all the mussels to move around. Drain, strain the cooking liquid and keep it for the soup. Detach the mussels from their shells and set aside the meat.

Heat oil and butter over a medium heat in a medium-sized saucepan. Add the leek, carrot and fennel, and stir for 5 minutes. Stir in the saffron, tomatoes and potato, and the strained mussel juice. Season with salt and pepper, and cook for 20 minutes.

Add the white fish to soup and cook over a low heat for 5 minutes. Blend the soup and fish until smooth. Add the cayenne and season to taste with salt and pepper. Add some boiling water if necessary, to thin the soup a little. Add mussels and reheat for 1 minute, then stir in the cream and garlic. Sprinkle with the chives and serve with toasted bread.

barbecued tuna steaks with a mustard and egg sauce

SERVES 4

5 tbsp olive oil

3 tsp hot Dijon mustard

1 tsp finely crushed black peppercorns

4 tuna steaks, each weighing about 150 g (about 5 oz) and 2 cm (1 in) thick

juice of 1 lemon

2 hard-boiled eggs

1 tbsp baby capers

3 tbsp finely chopped fresh coriander or parsley

salt and freshly ground black pepper

Mix 2 tablespoons of the oil with 1 teaspoon of the mustard. Press the crushed peppercorns onto the tuna steaks and brush with the oil and mustard mixture.

In a bowl, whisk the remaining mustard with the lemon juice and then, still whisking, slowly add remaining oil. Chop the eggs coarsely and add to the sauce with the capers and coriander. Season with salt and pepper.

Barbecue or pan-fry the tuna over a medium heat for about 2 minutes on each side. Season with salt and leave to rest for 3–4 minutes in a warm spot (not too hot) at the side of the barbecue. Serve tuna on individual plates with a little of the sauce spooned over the top.

baked coral trout with lemon grass

SERVES 4

a 1 kg (about 2 lb) coral trout

1 tbsp finely grated ginger root

1 clove garlic, finely chopped

1 tsp sesame oil

a 10 cm (4 in) piece of lemon grass, finely sliced

2 tbsp light soy sauce

juice of 2 limes

freshly ground black pepper

4 tbsp hot water

a few sprigs of coriander

For its firm flesh, coral trout is one of my favourite fish. If you cannot find lemon grass, use half a teaspoon of fennel seeds.

Preheat the oven to 200°C/400°F.

Make a few cuts 1 cm ($\frac{1}{2}$ in) deep and 2 cm (1 in) apart on both sides of the fish, at its thickest part. In a bowl combine the ginger, garlic, sesame oil, lemon grass, soy sauce, half the lime juice and a little black pepper. Lay the fish in an oiled oven tray and rub it all over with the marinade, putting a few lemon grass slices inside the fish. Pour in the hot water, cover the tray with foil and bake in the preheated oven for 20–30 minutes or until the fish flakes easily.

Serve the fish with the remaining lime juice squeezed over it, and garnished with coriander leaves.

rainbow trout

with a lemon and caper salsa

S ERVES 4

4 tbsp olive oil

2 sundried tomatoes

sea salt and freshly ground black pepper

1/2 medium-sized onion, finely chopped

4 rainbow trout, each weighing
about 250 g (about 9 oz)

juice of 2 lemons

1 tbsp baby capers

2 tbsp finely chopped fresh dill

The aroma of the trout barbecuing in a seasoning of tomato and onion is irresistible. And what a bonus if you have caught your own fish.

Purée the sundried tomatoes and half the olive oil in your smallest food processor jar. Season with salt and pepper, and mix in the chopped onion.

Make a few cuts in the thickest part of the fish and rub them over with the tomato mixture. Marinate for 1/2–2 hours in the fridge.

Cook the trout on a very clean barbecue for 4 minutes over a medium heat (don't disturb them during this time). Then carefully turn it over and cook for a further 4 minutes. Meanwhile, mix the lemon juice with remaining oil, the capers and the dill, and season with salt and pepper. Lift the fish carefully onto plates, spoon the sauce over the top and serve.

sweet chilli prawn kebabs with coriander

SERVES 4

1 tsp chilli paste, or more if you wish

2 tbsp vegetable oil

1 tbsp light soy sauce

2 tsp honey

$\frac{1}{2}$ tsp sesame oil

1 tbsp finely chopped fresh coriander leaves

salt and freshly ground black pepper

24 medium-sized green prawns, shelled and deveined

lemon or lime wedges for garnish

My travels in Asia have introduced me to new ideas for seasoning seafood. The combination of chilli, coriander, sesame oil and lemon is a particular favourite of mine.

Thoroughly combine the chilli paste, oil, soy sauce, honey, sesame oil and coriander in a bowl and season with salt and pepper. Add prawns and mix gently to coat them in the marinade. Cover with plastic wrap or foil, and marinate in the fridge for at least 20 minutes.

Thread two prawns onto each skewer. Barbecue the kebabs for about 1 minute on each side over a medium heat.

Serve immediately, with lemon wedges.

witlof salad with stilton and walnuts

SERVES 4

600 g (about 1 $\frac{1}{4}$ lb) very fresh witlof (Belgian endives)

1 tbsp red-wine vinegar

1 clove garlic, finely chopped

salt and freshly ground black pepper

3 tbsp olive oil or walnut oil

100 g (about 3 $\frac{1}{2}$ oz) finely chopped walnuts

150 g (about 5 oz) Stilton, cut into 1 cm ($\frac{1}{2}$ in) cubes

1 tbsp chopped parsley (optional)

A salad much loved by Europeans. Use Roquefort, or your favourite blue-vein cheese, if you can't get Stilton.

Separate the witlof leaves and wash them briefly in a large amount of cold water. Drain, and dry using a salad spinner.

In a salad bowl, thoroughly combine the vinegar, garlic, salt, pepper and oil. Add the walnuts, cheese and salad leaves. Toss the salad very gently before serving sprinkled with chopped parsley.

DELICACIES

of the sea

Prawns, oysters, scampi, salmon, John Dory—even the names inspire me. I adore the produce of the sea.

When I look back, I realise how lucky I was to work as a *commis* chef at Prunier, the famous Parisian seafood restaurant. I was only eighteen and Prunier was in its heyday. It was there I learned that what ultimately makes a great seafood dish is the freshness of its ingredients.

Wherever I have lived, I have taken the time to find a reliable fishmonger. There are several in every city and usually one or two in small towns and at the better markets. Selling fish is a demanding profession, for you have to be at the wholesale market early, ready to select your day's supply and then be back at the shop in time to open up. A good fishmonger does not necessarily sell a big range of fish. In fact, I prefer one that offers few varieties and where freshness is paramount. Try to cultivate a friendly relationship with a fishmonger, for this leads to good service. A true professional is always happy to clean, scale and fillet fish for you, advise you on the best buy of the day and even let you peel a prawn to test its freshness.

It is never worth buying fish that is anything less than very fresh. Fresh fish looks plump and has a firm texture. It has shiny, slippery skin, and the scales hold together closely. The eyes are usually clear and bulging, and the gills are pink. Don't buy fish more than one day before you plan to cook it, and avoid buying frozen fish if at all possible. Once home, put the fish in the coldest part of the refigerator. And when the time comes to cook it, remember that fish and seafood cook faster than meat and are very fragile, so handle gently and don't overcook. And always cook fish at the last minute, for it does not reheat well.

a tart of sardines

with olives

250 g (about 9 oz) puff pastry (page 175)

about 1 cup Italian-style tomato sauce (not too runny)

2 anchovy fillets, finely chopped

22 semi-dried olives, pitted and finely chopped

2 sprigs of lemon thyme

2 tbsp olive oil

salt and freshly ground black pepper

12–18 fresh sardine fillets

A superb summer entrée or light lunch. I was inspired to cook this dish after a visit to my favourite restaurant just outside Aix-en-Provence, Le Relais Ste. Victoire, where I have enjoyed some of the best Provençale cuisine. Use very fresh sardines, preferably filleted for you on the spot.

Preheat oven to 200°C/400°F.

Roll out the puff pastry to a 25 cm (10 in) circle about 3 mm ($\frac{1}{4}$ in) thick. Prick the pastry with a fork to minimise shrinkage. Line an oven sheet with baking paper then line this with the pastry.

In a bowl mix the tomato sauce with the chopped anchovies and one-third of the chopped olives. Spread a thin layer of this mixture over the centre of the pastry, leaving a 1 cm ($\frac{1}{2}$ in) margin around the edge. Bake in the preheated oven for about 15 minutes, or until the base is lightly browned.

Meanwhile, finely chop the thyme and mix with the olive oil. Season with salt and pepper, then coat the sardine fillets with this mixture. Arrange the sardines attractively on the prepared pastry, then bake in the preheated oven for a few minutes until the sardines are just cooked. Top with remaining chopped olives, and serve. (This tart is also delicious cold.)

butter-bean stew

with orange gremolata

Food for the gods. This dish was popular centuries ago and is also a food of the future. The butter bean has one of the most satisfying textures of any ingredient.

Place the beans in a large amount of cold water, cover and refrigerate for 12 hours. If possible, change the soaking water once or twice.

Tie the bay leaf, thyme and parsley together with kitchen string to make a bouquet garni. Drain the soaked beans and place in a medium-sized saucepan with the onion, 2 of the garlic cloves, the bouquet garni, tomato paste and tomato sauce. Cover with water and bring to the boil. Simmer for 1–1½ hours, until the beans are tender. (Do not add salt during the cooking as this toughens the beans.) Add a little extra boiling water during the cooking if necessary.

When the beans are cooked, discard the onion, garlic and bouquet garni. Season the beans with salt and pepper and just before serving stir in the remaining clove of garlic (chopped), the orange zest, chopped parsley and olive oil.

artichoke heart

and mushroom casserole

about 4 cups cold water

4 slices lemon, each about 1 cm ($\frac{1}{2}$ in) thick

8 large globe artichokes

2 tbsp olive oil

1 medium-sized onion, finely chopped

1 tsp coriander seeds

10 fennel seeds

300 g (about 11 oz) small button mushrooms

1 tsp tomato paste

$\frac{1}{3}$ cup dry white wine

4 medium-sized tomatoes, diced

salt and freshly ground black pepper

2 tbsp chopped parsley

This vegetable dish is redolent of the flavours of Provence. The delicacy of the artichokes makes it an ideal entrée for a special summer occasion.

Pour the water into a large bowl with 2 slices of lemon. Cut each of the remaining lemon slices into 8 pieces.

Using a paring knife, cut off the artichoke stalks. Also cut off the top part of the artichoke leaves, leaving about 3 cm (1½ in) of the base. Carefully trim the remaining leaves to expose the heart. Use a spoon to scoop out the hairy part of the choke from the centre of the heart, then place the hearts in the bowl of water and rub them with the lemon slices to prevent discolouration.

Heat the oil in a large pan and gently fry the onion over a medium heat for about 3 minutes. Quarter the artichoke hearts and add them to the pan with the coriander and fennel seeds, stirring for 1 minute. Add the mushrooms and cook for 1 minute, then stir in the tomato paste, wine, tomatoes and reserved lemon pieces. Season with salt and pepper and cook over a low heat, stirring occasionally, for about 15 minutes or until the hearts are tender. Stir in the chopped parsley and serve hot or cold.

LIBRE SERVICE
proxi
LIVRAISON A DOMICILE
42.23.24.18
SANDWICHES
GLACES
BAR DES P.T.T
Phénix
BOISSONS
DE L'HOTEL DE VI

gratin of potato and witlof
with blue cheese

500 g (about 1 lb) potatoes

salt

3 medium-sized witlof (Belgian endives)

20 g (about ⅔ oz) butter

⅓ cup milk

2 tbsp cream

150 g (about 5 oz) blue-vein cheese
(not too sharp)

freshly ground black pepper

4 tbsp fresh breadcrumbs

Serve this either on its own, with grilled meat or fish, or with roast chicken, accompanied by a crisp green salad and your favourite bottle of wine. The bitterness of the witlof and the sweetness of the cheese make a superb flavour contrast.

Place the unpeeled potatoes in a saucepan, cover with cold water, season with salt and cook until just done. Drain.

Preheat the oven to 160°C/320°F. Wash the witlof and cut the leaves into strips. Heat the butter in a large frying pan and cook the witlof over a medium heat for about 10 minutes or until soft.

Bring the milk and cream to the boil in a large saucepan. Peel the drained potatoes, cut them into pieces and add to the hot milk mixture. Add the cheese and then mash everything together, using a fork. (Don't overdo it.) Add the witlof, season to taste with salt and pepper, and mix until just combined. Spoon into a greased gratin dish, sprinkle with breadcrumbs and bake in the preheated oven for about 15 minutes.

radicchio salad with a pesto dressing

SERVES 6

2–3 heads of fresh, crisp radicchio

juice of ½ lemon

about 50 basil leaves

2 tbsp pine nuts

2 cloves garlic

1 tbsp grated parmesan

2 tbsp olive oil

salt and freshly ground black pepper

3 hard-boiled eggs, quartered

Radicchio is one of the most colourful salad leaves. It is also one of the most strongly flavoured, with a hint of bitterness. It is delicious with a basil and pine-nut dressing, which can be prepared 2–3 days ahead and stored in an air-tight container in the fridge.

Separate radicchio leaves, and wash and dry them, tearing large leaves into smaller pieces. Place in a large salad bowl.

In a food processor, blend the lemon juice, basil, pine nuts and garlic to a paste. Add the parmesan, oil, salt and pepper, and blend till well combined. Toss dressing with salad leaves and top with quartered eggs. Serve immediately.

marinated capsicums with fetta

A most delicious Mediterranean summer salad with bright colour highlights.

SERVES 4

1 green capsicum

1 yellow capsicum

1 red capsicum

2 cloves garlic, crushed

4 tbsp olive oil

12 basil leaves

salt and freshly ground black pepper

120 g (about 4 oz) fetta cheese

20 baby olives, e.g. niçoise

Preheat the griller. Put the whole capsicums on an oven rack resting in an oven tray, and place under the grill with the capsicums about 5 cm (2 in) from the heat. Cook until the skins start to bubble and darken, then turn the capsicums over and continue to cook until all sides are done (10–20 minutes).

Place capsicums in a large plastic bag, close it with a twist tie and leave for 15 minutes. Alternatively, wrap them in foil. When the skins have softened, cut the capsicums in half, remove the seeds and peel, and trim the stalk end. If necessary, dry them with kitchen paper. Cut each capsicum half into 3 or 4 strips and place in a bowl with the garlic, oil, basil, salt and pepper. Leave to marinate for at least 2–3 hours.

When ready to serve, drain the capsicums and place them on a dish. Top with broken or cubed pieces of fetta and the olives and serve.

chicken fillets with a tomato salsa

5 tbsp olive oil

2 tsp finely chopped fresh oregano

2 tsp finely chopped fresh lemon thyme

salt and freshly ground black pepper

6 chicken fillets, skin off

24 cherry tomatoes, quartered

juice of 2 lemons

1 tbsp baby capers (optional)

1 tbsp basil, cut into strips

1 clove garlic, finely chopped

A simple but flavoursome dish. The sauce can be served hot or cold. Avoid overcooking the chicken, which needs no more than 5 minutes on each side.

Mix 2 tablespoons of the olive oil with the oregano and lemon thyme. Season with pepper and brush over the chicken fillets. (If you have time, cover the chicken and marinate for 2 hours in the fridge.)

Barbecue the chicken over a medium heat for about 5 minutes on each side. Season with salt and pepper and rest the fillets in a warm spot at the side of the barbecue for 5–10 minutes before serving.

Place the tomatoes and remaining oil in a small pan and heat through. Season with salt and pepper, then stir in the lemon juice, capers, basil and garlic. Spoon this sauce over chicken and serve with a range of salads.

mediterranean barbecued quail

SERVES 4

4 medium-sized quail

4 tbsp olive oil

¼ tsp aniseed

2 tbsp finely chopped fresh basil

1 clove garlic, finely chopped

1 tsp dried oregano

freshly ground black pepper

salt

1 lemon, quartered

A finger-licking treat and one of the best ways to cook quail. The aniseed and basil give it a sophisticated summer flavour.

Using kitchen scissors, cut each quail in half. Remove any organs left inside such as the heart and lungs.

Combine olive oil, aniseed, basil, garlic, oregano and pepper in a bowl. Add quail halves and rub them all over with the marinade. Cover with plastic wrap and refrigerate for at least 2 hours.

Barbecue quail over a medium heat for about 4–5 minutes on each side. Season with salt and serve with lemon wedges.

chicken satay

MAKES 8 SATAY STICKS

a 10 cm (4 in) piece of lemon grass,
finely sliced

2 tbsp light soy sauce

1 tsp sugar

2 cloves garlic, very finely chopped

2 tsp ground cumin

$\frac{1}{2}$ tsp ground turmeric

2 tsp ground coriander

$\frac{1}{2}$ tsp chilli paste

1 tbsp vegetable oil

600 g (about 1$\frac{1}{4}$ lb) boneless chicken meat

1 lemon, cut into wedges

spicy peanut sauce (optional, page 170)

Satays are especially popular with children. They are also a simple way to add interest to barbecued meats. If you use wooden sticks, soak them in cold water for 20 minutes beforehand to prevent them burning.

Mix lemon grass, soy sauce, sugar, garlic, cumin, turmeric, coriander, chilli and oil in a bowl. Cut chicken into strips about 2 cm (1 in) long and 1.5 cm ($\frac{3}{4}$ in) wide. Add chicken to the marinade and mix well. Cover with plastic wrap and refrigerate for about 3 hours.

Thread the chicken pieces onto satay sticks, discarding the lemon grass. Barbecue over a medium heat for a few minutes on each side. Serve satays either on their own, with lemon juice or a peanut sauce.

salad of baby fennel with eggs and olives

SERVES 6

600–800 g (about 1$\frac{1}{4}$–1$\frac{3}{4}$ lb) baby
fennel bulbs

about 20 small black olives

juice of 1 large lemon

salt and freshly ground black pepper

3 tbsp olive oil

$\frac{1}{2}$ red onion, diced

2 tbsp finely chopped parsley

2 hard-boiled eggs, coarsely chopped

Raw fennel is one of the most refreshing ingredients. The flavour reminds me of holidays in Italy. If baby fennel is unavailable, use the smallest, freshest-looking bulbs you can find.

Cut off the fennel stems and any damaged leaves. Halve each bulb and trim the root end. Wash fennel and cut into 5–10 mm ($\frac{1}{4}$–$\frac{1}{2}$ in) slices. Place in a large bowl with the olives.

Place the lemon juice, salt and pepper in a mixing bowl. Add the oil, onion, parsley and eggs, and stir until just combined. Spoon dressing over the fennel, toss gently, and serve.

CHEESE —

fromage — formaggio

I was born in a cheese paradise. This might sound one-eyed, but if you know France and love cheese you'll understand. In France they have been making cheese for centuries and it's no exaggeration to say that it's almost worth going there for the cheese alone: Brie, Camembert, Roquefort, Chèvre, Pont l'Evêque—the list is endless. But, of course, France is by no means the exclusive producer of great cheeses and many other countries, including most European nations, Australia and the United States also produce wonderful varieties.

Selecting cheese for your table is a matter of personal taste but it is fun to provide a choice. This might be of textures (soft, hard, crumbly) or of flavours (sharp, mild, aromatic). Or you might simply serve the classics, such as an English Stilton, an Australian mature Cheddar, a French Brie, an Italian Parmesan, a Swiss Gruyère and a Dutch Gouda. Buy cheese from a specialist cheese store or good deli which offers farmhouse produce rather than mass-produced cheese. Good retailers will let you sample the cheese and will make recommendations, for cheese is seasonal. They will wrap your purchases carefully in paper, which won't stick to the cheese and prevents spoiling.

Bread is my favourite accompaniment for cheese, especially baguette, sourdough, wholegrain or walnut bread. Fresh fruit also goes well with cheese: I love pears, apples and grapes, and sometimes serve dried grapes and walnuts, hazelnuts or almonds. Always present cheese whole or in generous wedges, providing one knife per cheese so as not to mix the flavours. Make sure also to serve water and a good wine.

spicy duck fillet

on rocket leaves

20 black peppercorns, finely crushed

20 coriander seeds, finely crushed

20 fennel seeds, each cut into 2–3 pieces

1 tsp coarse sea salt

1 tbsp olive oil

4 duck fillets, boned

1 tbsp raspberry vinegar

salt and freshly ground black pepper

2 shallots, finely chopped

3 tbsp walnut oil

200 g (about 7 oz) rocket, well washed

2 tbsp finely chopped walnuts

a few sprigs of chervil (optional)

I often order duck in a good restaurant as I have a weakness for its exotic sweetness. Try this great dish: it's so simple and so delicious.

Combine peppercorns, coriander seeds, fennel seeds and sea salt on a plate and rub into the skin of the duck. Preheat the oven to 180°C/350°F.

Heat olive oil in a non-stick pan and cook duck pieces, skin-side down, for 5 minutes. Turn duck over and cook for another minute. Transfer to an ovenproof dish and roast in the preheated oven for 10 minutes. Remove from oven and rest for 10 minutes before slicing it very thinly.

In a bowl mix the vinegar with a little salt and pepper and stir in the shallots and the walnut oil. Toss gently with the rocket leaves. Arrange the dressed leaves on plates and top with the thinly sliced duck meat. Sprinkle walnuts on top, garnish with chervil and serve.

indian-style butterflied lamb

Marinated and then slow-cooked, the lamb is delicately spicy and tender. Serve it sliced very thinly.

1 tbsp finely grated ginger root

2 cloves garlic, finely chopped

2 tsp garam masala

1 tsp ground cumin

1 tsp aniseed

2 tbsp vegetable oil

1 tbsp lemon juice

1 tsp hot chilli paste

a 1.8 kg (about 4 lb) leg of lamb, deboned and butterflied

salt

a handful of coriander leaves

lemon wedges for garnish

In a bowl combine the ginger, garlic, garam masala, cumin, aniseed, oil, lemon juice and chilli paste. Rub this mixture all over the trimmed lamb. Place meat on a plate, cover with foil and marinate in the fridge for 1–4 hours.

Preheat the barbecue to low and place lamb on the grill. (If the heat is too high the meat will burn before it's even half-cooked.) Cook the meat for 15 minutes, then turn it over and cook on the second side for 10–15 minutes, depending on how well done you like your meat.

Cut lamb into 1 cm ($\frac{1}{2}$ in) slices, season with salt and serve garnished with coriander leaves and lemon wedges.

barbecued cutlets with north african flavours

Serves 6

The cuisine of North Africa is slowly being discovered by the rest of the world. It is food of the sun punctuated with spices.

4 racks of lamb, each with 6 cutlets

4 tbsp olive oil

1 tbsp finely chopped fresh mint

1 tsp harissa (a North African chilli paste)

2 tsp ground cumin

$\frac{1}{4}$ tsp ground cinnamon

1 tsp tomato paste

$\frac{1}{4}$ tsp freshly ground black pepper

Cut each lamb rack into three double cutlets. Trim meat of any fat.

In a large bowl mix the olive oil, mint, harissa, cumin, cinnamon, tomato paste and pepper. Rub the meat all over with this spicy preparation, then cover meat with plastic wrap and leave to marinate for 1–2 hours in the fridge.

Barbecue over a medium heat for about 4–5 minutes on each side. Allow the meat to rest for a few minutes before serving.

dinner
parties

There is much more to a dinner party than meets the eye (or, for that matter, the stomach). Like many other cooks, in the past I was often guilty of neglecting myself and our guests by spending half the evening in the kitchen. Fortunately, times have changed and most people no longer expect those large three or four-course meals that we all used to produce so painstakingly. Nowadays the answer is to cook a lovely dish or two from the freshest and most interesting ingredients, and complement this with pre-prepared foods for nibbles, antipasto, salads and dessert.

Happily, food retailers have realised that people—especially the ones who do the cooking—want to entertain more simply. We can now purchase special cuts of meat, such as veal chops, beef fillet or lamb loin, which have been portioned and trimmed of fat and are ready to cook. Poulterers and fishmongers are equally eager to satisfy their customers and offer (usually prepare on demand) quick-cook cuts and portions which only need a few minutes' cooking. More demanding dishes like stews and casseroles can be prepared well in advance, leaving the cook free to share a relaxed first drink with the guests.

There's no place like home to enjoy the company of good friends. And with a little planning and selectiveness, the tradition of the dinner party can live on.

veal chops

with orange gremolata

SERVES 4

4 veal chops, about 2.5 cm (1 in) thick

salt and freshly ground black pepper

2 tbsp olive oil

20 g (about $^2/_3$ oz) butter

2 tbsp dry white wine

2 tbsp orange juice

6 tbsp beef or veal stock (page 164)

2 tsp cornflour mixed with 2 tbsp water

2 cloves garlic, finely chopped

2 tbsp chopped parsley

1 tbsp chopped fresh basil

finely grated zest of 1 orange

finely grated zest of $^1/_2$ lemon

In Europe veal is a highlight at special dinners, where much care is taken to avoid overcooking the meat and to keep it moist.

Preheat the oven to warm (100°C/210°F). Season the veal with salt and pepper.

Heat the oil and half the butter in a non-stick frying pan over a medium heat and cook the chops for about 3–4 minutes on each side. Transfer chops to a plate, cover with foil and place in the warm oven while you make the sauce.

Add the wine to the same pan, bring to the boil and reduce by half. Add the orange juice and boil for 20 seconds before adding the stock. Return to the boil and stir in the cornflour mixture to thicken the sauce. Simmer for 2 minutes and stir in the garlic, parsley, basil, orange and lemon zest, and remaining butter. Season sauce to taste, pour over veal and serve. Lovely with polenta or pasta.

veal fillets

with wild mushroom sauce

SERVES 4

200 g (about 7 oz) wild mushrooms, cleaned

600 g (about 1¼ lb) veal fillet

salt and freshly ground black pepper

1 tbsp vegetable oil

20 g (about ⅔ oz) butter

3 shallots, finely chopped

1 clove garlic, finely chopped

1½ tbsp dry white wine, e.g. chardonnay,
riesling

⅓ cup veal stock (page 164)

4 tbsp cream

2 tbsp chopped parsley

Veal goes particularly well with mushrooms, as the mild flavour of the meat allows the mushrooms to star. This is a glorious dish for autumn, when you can buy or gather fresh wild mushrooms. Out of season, you can use dried wild mushrooms such as porcini or chanterelles.

Trim off any hard or damaged parts of the mushrooms then wash the mushrooms briefly in cold water. Slice or quarter larger ones. Cut the veal into slices 1.5 cm (about ¾ in) thick.

Season the veal with salt and pepper. Heat the oil and half the butter in a non-stick frying pan and cook veal over a medium heat for about 3 minutes on each side. Transfer veal to a warm plate, cover with foil and place in a warm oven (100°C/210°F). Add the shallots to pan and stir for 30 seconds. Add mushrooms and remaining butter, and cook over a high heat for 2 minutes or until the mushrooms are soft. Stir in garlic, then spoon the mushrooms over the meat . Cover again and return to the warm oven while you make the sauce.

Add the wine to the pan and bring to the boil. Add the stock, return to the boil and then add the cream. Boil for 30 seconds and season to taste. Spoon the sauce over mushrooms and meat, sprinkle with parsley and serve.

veal shank couscous

with carrots

S ERVES 4–6

4 veal shanks, left whole or cut as for
osso buco

1 tbsp harissa (a North African chilli paste)

salt and freshly ground black pepper

1 medium-sized onion, sliced

2 tbsp olive oil

1$\frac{1}{2}$ tbsp ground cumin

$\frac{1}{4}$ tsp fennel seeds

2 tbsp tomato paste, diluted in a little water

4 medium-sized tomatoes, diced

2 green capsicums, sliced lengthwise into 8

6 medium-sized carrots

1 cup canned chick peas, drained

about 2 cups couscous

1 cup fresh coriander leaves

extra harissa for the table

A classic North African dish of coarse wheat semolina served with vegetables, meat and chick peas. It is one of my favourite treats to share with family or friends in a relaxed atmosphere.

Rub the veal shanks with the harissa and season with salt and pepper. Place in a large saucepan with the onion, olive oil, 1 tbsp of the cumin, the fennel seeds, diluted tomato paste, tomatoes and capsicum. Cover with cold water, bring to the boil and simmer for 30 minutes. Add carrots and cook for a further 15 minutes. Add the chickpeas and cook until the carrots are soft and the meat is easily detached from the bone. This part of the dish can be done in advance.

Follow the instructions on the couscous pack or, for best results, first place the couscous in a fine strainer and run cold water over it for 2–3 minutes. Then use a damp cloth or muslin to line the perforated compartment of your steamer. Put in the wet couscous and bring the water in the steamer to the boil. Steam the couscous, uncovered, for about 15 minutes or until the grains are soft and hot.

Stir the remaining cumin into the veal stew and season to taste with salt and pepper. Spoon the couscous onto a large platter or into a bowl, and spoon about one quarter of the juices over it with some of the vegetables. Serve the remaining vegetables, meat and juice in a separate bowl. Sprinkle with the coriander leaves and provide extra harissa on the table.

roast pheasant in pastry

with spinach and pears

This is the kind of dish I imagine might have been served to the kings of France. I served it to many happy clients in the days when I used to cook for private dinners. You can make your own puff pastry, or buy it from a baker.

SERVES 4

200 g (about 7 oz) puff pastry

1 egg yolk mixed with 1 tsp water

1 tbsp vegetable oil

1 pheasant, weighing about 1 kg (about 2 lb)

salt and freshly ground black pepper

300 g (about 11 oz) baby spinach leaves

2 just-ripe pears

1 tbsp cream

50 g (almost 2 oz) butter

2 tsp plain flour

2 tbsp dry madeira or ¼ cup dry white wine

1 cup strong chicken stock (page 165)

Preheat oven to 250°C/500°F. Roll out the pastry to about 4 mm thick, then cut into 4 rounds each about 10 cm in diameter.

Prick holes in the pastry with a fork. Brush the pastry with the egg yolk and water, and use a fork to make a criss-cross pattern on top. Bake in the preheated oven for 5 minutes then lower the temperature to 180°C/350°F and cook until pastry is golden-brown on top and lightly coloured underneath (this takes 15–20 minutes). Remove pastry from oven and put aside.

Heat the oil in a small, thick roasting tray. When it is hot, put in the pheasant and brown it on both sides. Season with salt and pepper, and roast in the preheated oven for about 25 minutes.

Meanwhile, wash the spinach and cook in its own steam in a covered saucepan. Peel and quarter pears and cut each quarter into two long halves. Place pear pieces in a saucepan with the cream, stir gently and boil for 20 seconds. Drain the spinach and gently mix it in with the pears. Season with salt and pepper.

Transfer the roasted pheasant to a plate and cover with foil. Melt a small knob of the butter in the roasting tray over a medium heat and stir in the flour for 20 seconds. Whisk in madeira and chicken stock, bring to the boil and reduce liquid by half.

Carve the pheasant. Remove the flesh from the bones and cut into thin, bite-sized slices. Add the pheasant slices and remaining butter to the sauce, and season to taste.

Reheat the pastry rounds, then cut each round through horizontally. Place a little of the spinach and pear mixture on the pastry bases. Add a few slices of pheasant with its sauce, top with pastry lids and serve.

baked quail

with a sauce of orange-blossom honey and ginger

S E R V E S 4

a 3 cm (1½ in) piece of ginger root

1 tsp vegetable oil

50 g (almost 2 oz) butter

1 tbsp orange-blossom honey or other honey

8 medium-sized quail

2 cloves garlic, finely chopped

¼ tsp hot chilli paste

1 cup finely diced carrot, 5 mm (¼ in) square

1 cup finely diced celery, 5 mm (¼ in) square

2 tbsp soy sauce

1½ cups strong chicken stock (page 165)

salt and freshly ground black pepper

An east-meets-west recipe, in which tender quail are bathed in a sweet and spicy sauce. Provide your guests with finger bowls so they can be relaxed about sucking the bones.

Peel and grate the ginger.

Heat the oil and half the butter in a large saucepan. Stir in the honey and brown the quail over a medium heat. Lower heat and add half the garlic, two-thirds of the ginger, then the chilli paste, carrot, celery and soy sauce. Cover pan with foil and then a lid and cook for 10 minutes. Turn the quail over and cook, covered, for a further 5 minutes. Transfer quail to a serving dish and keep in a warm oven at 100°C/210°F.

Add the stock to the vegetables in the pan and bring to the boil. Reduce by half, then stir in the remaining ginger, garlic and butter. Season sauce to taste with salt and pepper and spoon over the quail. Serve with steamed spinach.

roast rack of lamb

with rosemary and baby spinach

4 racks of lamb, each with 4 cutlets

3 tbsp olive oil

1 tbsp finely chopped rosemary

½ tsp ground paprika

½ tsp chilli paste

2 small cloves garlic, finely chopped

salt and freshly ground black pepper

600 g (about 1¼ lb) fresh baby
spinach, washed

2 tbsp butter

2 tbsp freshly grated parmesan (optional)

After living for eighteen months in Provence where the lamb is superb, I came to realise that rosemary and roast lamb are made for each other, particularly if both are young.

Preheat the oven to 180°C/350°F.

Trim all excess fat from the lamb. In a bowl, combine the olive oil, rosemary, paprika, chilli paste, half the garlic and a little salt and pepper. Rub the lamb all over with this marinade.

Place the meat on a rack sitting in an oven tray and roast in the preheated oven for 15–20 minutes. Remove from oven, cover with foil and leave to rest for at least 5 minutes.

Meanwhile, place the spinach in a large saucepan. Cover pan and cook until the spinach has wilted. Drain, squeeze out the excess water then chop spinach roughly. Heat the butter in a pan and stir in the remaining garlic. Add the spinach to reheat, and season with salt and pepper.

Carve the lamb. Place spinach on plates and top with the cutlets. Sprinkle parmesan cheese over, season with extra black pepper and serve.

lamb shanks

in an orange and herb sauce

SERVES 4

2 tbsp olive oil

4 trimmed lamb shanks

3 sprigs of thyme

$1/2$ medium-sized brown onion, cut into small pieces

1 stick of celery, chopped

grated zest of 1 orange

2 tbsp white wine

3 tomatoes, chopped

2 cloves garlic, chopped

3 medium-sized carrots, cut into 3 cm ($1^1/2$ in) lengths

salt and freshly ground black pepper

1 tbsp finely chopped fresh basil

1 tbsp finely chopped parsley

$1/2$ tbsp chopped fresh mint (optional)

Baked lamb shanks make a superb winter main course. The sweetness of the meat is further enriched by the tangy orange zest and aromatic herbs.

Preheat the oven to 150°C/300°F.

Heat the oil in an ovenproof casserole and brown the shanks all over for a few minutes. Add the thyme, onion, celery and orange zest, and stir for 2 minutes. Then add the wine, tomatoes, garlic and carrots, season with salt and pepper, and stir well. Bring to a simmer, cover and place in the preheated oven. Turn the meat over after 1 hour and then again 30 minutes later. Cook the shanks 2 hours in total, until the meat falls away from the bones

Remove the meat and carrots from the dish, cover them with foil and place in a warm oven. Strain the sauce into a small saucepan, adding some boiling water from the kettle if it is too thick. Stir in the basil, parsley and mint and season to taste. Spoon the sauce over the lamb and carrots, then serve.

THE GREENGROCER

You know when you are in a good fruit and vegetable shop. Everything is displayed with great care and attention. The green vegetables are crisp and tender, the root vegetables full and firm. There is a good selection of salad greens and herbs, often including new and unusual varieties. The fruits are ripe, or almost ripe. The citrus fruits are firm and heavy, the berries look luscious and are deeply hued, the stone fruits smell irresistible. It's obvious which fruits are in season— their heady aromas fill the air. A visit to the greengrocer inspires me tremendously—it's a feast for the eyes that urges me to create new dishes and puts me in a happy mood for the rest of the day.

Of all foods, vegetables offer the greatest variety of flavours, textures, colours and nutrition. At home we make the most of seasonal treats—perhaps asparagus with a hollandaise sauce, artichokes with a dressing of walnut oil and lemon, young sugar peas or tender bok choy in light stir-fries, or broad beans in a hearty Mediterranean stew. My repertoire of vegetable dishes has been inspired by Asian and Mediterranean cooks and cookbooks. I realise that it is often in societies where less meat is eaten, such as India, China, Italy and North Africa, that the most interesting vegetable dishes are created.

Treat wonderful vegetables with respect and avoid undercooking or overcooking them. Experiment with herbs and spices you have not used before, and with new cooking techniques. Try stir-frying or roasting (brush sweet potatoes with vegetable oil, chilli paste and a pinch of curry powder), stewing mixed Mediterranean vegetables, or steam some greens. Devise some exciting salads. *C'est si bon*—and so good *for* us!

Artichaud
Pays
kg
Girolles
990
le kg

double sirloin steak with a wine sauce

2 pieces of trimmed sirloin, each weighing 300 g (about 11 oz)

2 tsp crushed black peppercorns.

1 tbsp vegetable oil

1 tbsp butter

3 medium-sized shallots, finely chopped

1 tsp plain flour

1/3 cup good red wine

3/4 cup beef stock (page 164)

salt and freshly ground black pepper

The texture of a juicy piece of sirloin is irresistible to meat-lovers. You'll enjoy this dish more if you drink the same red wine that you used in the cooking.

Preheat the oven to 120°C/250°F. Season meat with crushed pepper and rub it in.

Heat oil in a frying pan and cook meat for about 3 minutes on each side. Transfer meat to a dish and place in the preheated oven. Add half the butter to frying pan, add the shallots and stir over a low heat for 3 minutes. Stir in flour, add the wine, increase heat and boil until the wine has reduced by two-thirds. Add stock, return to the boil and cook for a further 3 minutes. Season with salt and pepper, and stir in remaining butter.

Remove meat from oven, season with salt and cut each piece into 6 slices. Place three slices on each plate, spoon sauce over and serve with mashed potatoes and steamed green beans.

grilled rump steak with pistounade provençale

2 sprigs of thyme, chopped

3 tbsp virgin olive oil

4 pieces of trimmed rump steak, each 2.5 cm (1 in) thick and weighing about 150 g (5 oz)

freshly ground black pepper

80 g (about 3 oz) pitted green olives

1 tbsp pine nuts

2 small cloves garlic

1/2 cup fresh basil leaves

a pinch of cayenne

The fragrance of the pistounade, a paste of green olives and basil, is divine. It is delicious spread over a hot steak, especially when served with a good French bread.

Mix the thyme with half the oil and season with a little pepper. Rub this mixture all over the meat, cover, and refrigerate until 10 minutes before cooking (but not for longer than a few hours).

In a food processor, blend the olives, pine nuts, garlic, basil and remaining oil almost to a purée. Season with cayenne and extra black pepper. Place in a bowl, cover with plastic wrap and refrigerate until required.

Barbecue the steaks, or pan-fry them, for 1–3 minutes on each side (depending on how you like your meat). Transfer to hot plates and spread with a thin layer of the pistounade. Serve immediately.

boeuf à la ficelle

S E R V E S 4

6 cups rich beef stock (page 164)

12 baby carrots

8 baby turnips, or 2 medium-sized turnips, quartered

1 red capsicum, cut lengthwise into 8

4 baby leeks, or 1 medium leek, cut lengthwise into 4

4 pieces of beef fillet from the middle, each weighing

150 g (about 5 oz)

freshly ground black pepper

about 8 sprigs of coriander for garnish

mustard and sea salt for the table

A classic dish of French bourgeois cuisine. The tenderness of the beef, the colour of the baby vegetables and the strong yet delicate flavours of the broth are to die for. The secret lies in the quality of the stock—if you use a commercial stock, try improving it with fresh vegetables. If you have time, make your own bouillon and taste the difference.

Bring the stock to the boil. Add the carrots, turnips, capsicum and leeks, and cook until tender. Remove vegetables and keep warm in a pan with a little of the broth, over a very low heat.

Tie each beef slice in a circle with 2 rounds of kitchen string to keep it firm during cooking. Place in the simmering broth and leave for about 5–8 minutes, according to how well done you like your meat.

Remove the meat and place each slice in a hot deep plate. Cut the strings and season the meat with black pepper. Arrange the vegetables around and on top of the meat and pour a ladleful of broth over. Garnish with the coriander sprigs and serve with mustard and sea salt.

avocado and rocket salad with a light curry dressing

S E R V E S 4

1 just-ripe avocado

2 medium-sized ripe tomatoes

1/2 tbsp balsamic or red wine vinegar

2 pinches of curry powder

salt and freshly ground black pepper

2 tbsp olive oil

a few black olives (optional)

250 g (about 9 oz) rocket, well washed and dried

Perfect with roast meat or grilled fish or meat. The small amount of curry powder gives a subtle spiciness which does not overwhelm the dressing.

Halve the avocado and remove the stone. Peel the flesh and cut into bite-sized pieces. Wash the tomatoes, remove the seeds and cut each tomato into 8 segments.

Combine the vinegar, curry powder and some salt and pepper in a salad bowl. Whisk in the olive oil.

Gently toss avocado, tomato and olives in the dressing. Add rocket and toss gently again just before serving.

wild mushroom risotto

SERVES 4

4 cups strong chicken stock (page 165) or
vegetable stock (page 167)

3 tbsp olive oil

½ brown onion, finely chopped

1 small carrot, finely chopped

a 15 cm (6 in) stick of celery, finely chopped

300 g (about 11 oz) arborio rice (Italian
round-grain rice)

300 g (about 11 oz) wild mushrooms of your
choice, or 40 g (about 1½ oz) dried
wild mushrooms

50 g (almost 2 oz) butter

salt and freshly ground black pepper

3 tbsp chopped parsley

1 tbsp freshly grated parmesan

Nature teases us constantly—it makes us wait impatiently for our favourite seasonal foods, like wild mushrooms. But it's worth the wait. If you use dried mushrooms, soak them in warm water for about half an hour and then squeeze out the moisture. Rinse them in cold water and add them at the same time as you would the fresh ones.

Bring the stock to a simmer in a saucepan.

Heat 1 tablespoon of the oil in a large saucepan and gently fry the onion, carrot and celery for 3 minutes. Add the rice and stir well for about a minute. Add about a cup of the stock and bring to a low simmer, still stirring. When almost all the stock has been absorbed, add another cupful and continue to cook, stirring occasionally. Continue adding stock in this way until the rice is cooked but still firm in the centre. You should have enough stock: if not, add some boiling water.

Clean the mushrooms and cut into bite-sized pieces. Five minutes before the rice is ready, heat the remaining oil and half the butter in a frying pan and cook the mushrooms over a high heat until soft. Season with salt and pepper, and stir in the parsley. Gently fold the mushrooms into the risotto and add the remaining butter and the parmesan. Taste and correct the seasoning if necessary. At this point, the risotto should be creamy but not runny. Turn off the heat, cover the pan with a lid and leave to rest for 3 minutes before serving. Follow it with a mixed green salad.

vegetables
with ginger and chilli

200 g (about 7 oz) Chinese broccoli

2 heads of bok choy

200 g (about 7 oz) Chinese cabbage

100 g (about $3^{1}/_{2}$ oz) snow peas

2 tbsp peanut oil

4 slices ginger root, each 2 mm (about $^{1}/_{8}$ in) thick

1 small red chilli, finely sliced

1 clove garlic, crushed

2 tbsp light soy sauce

$^{1}/_{2}$ tsp sesame oil

freshly ground black pepper

4 spring onions, sliced

This looks wonderful presented on a large platter in the centre of the table. Occasionally, I serve it with roast duck, pork or chicken bought from an Asian take-away shop.

Remove any damaged or blemished parts from the broccoli, bok choy and cabbage, then cut them into bite-sized pieces. Top and tail the snow peas.

Bring about 8 cups of water to the boil in a wok. Add the vegetables, return to the boil and cook for 1 minute. Drain.

Dry the wok, then add the oil over a high heat and stir in the ginger, chilli and garlic. Add the drained vegetables and stir-fry for 3–4 minutes until they are tender. Add the soy sauce and sesame oil and season with pepper. Stir well and serve sprinkled with spring onions.

tempura of green sugar pea, asparagus and eggplant

This is an elegant and original way of serving vegetables. For special occasions, I use sugar peas, asparagus and eggplant, which go especially well with grilled fish or poultry. But you can use other vegetables such as zucchini, capsicum, broccoli and cauliflower.

Choose unblemished sugar peas. Wash them, but don't top or tail them. Use only the tips of the asparagus cut into 7 cm (about 2½ in) lengths and then washed. (Use the offcuts later in a soup.)

Dry the sugar peas and asparagus, using a towel or kitchen paper.

Cut the eggplants into quarters lengthwise.

Combine the chilled water and the egg in a bowl. Whisk in the flour, cornflour, baking powder, salt and cayenne.

Heat the oil in a deep-fryer to 180°C/350°F. In small batches, dip the sugar peas, asparagus tips and eggplant quarters into the batter: the batter should only coat them lightly. Drop them into the hot oil and fry for 2–3 minutes until the batter is golden. Drain on kitchen paper and serve immediately, perhaps with a sweet chilli sauce for dipping.

HERBS

of youth

Fine herbs add a natural, joyful freshness to food. A bland pasta is enlivened by the simple addition of finely snipped basil. A sprinkle of chopped chives or dill lifts and refreshes a seafood salad. And coriander leaves or spring onions scattered over steamed vegetables really make a difference.

All good cooks agree that herbs should be used fresh, and the best herbs I have ever tasted are those I have hand-picked from the gardens attached to the many domestic kitchens in which I have cooked. My father was a genius for growing vegetables and herbs, and I have the sweetest youthful memories of being dispatched to the garden, scissors in hand, by my mother or grandmother to collect some herbs which seconds later were thrown into the cooking pot or sprinkled over pan-fried meat or a salad. At home in France, Papa continues to grow parsley, chives, bay leaves, thyme, mint, sorrel and rosemary.

During my chef's apprenticeship on the Loire Valley the restaurant gardener grew as many seasonal herbs as possible. Our faithful clients knew just when it was worth making the drive of several hours in order to sample the house speciality—the renowned fricassée of free-range chicken with tarragon. Twenty-five years later the flavour of that dish still lingers in my memory. Herbs give a signature to a dish like no other group of ingredients can, perhaps with the exception of a few individual foods like truffles, lemons, some spices and chocolates.

Most herbs are plentiful in spring and early summer. Harvest them by cutting neatly with a knife or scissors; in summer, gather them in the morning before the sun gets too hot.

gratin dauphinois

1 kg (about 2 lb) potatoes

salt and freshly ground black pepper

2 cloves garlic, finely chopped

1 tbsp butter

2 cups full-cream milk

3 tbsp cream

100 g (about 3½ oz) grated gruyère cheese

2 tbsp chopped parsley

Rich and satisfying, this is the favourite French potato dish (after French fries) for special occasions. Serve it on its own, plus a green salad or with roasted or grilled meat.

Preheat the oven to 180°C/350°F.

Peel and wash the potatoes, halving large ones lengthwise, and then cut into slices about 3 mm (⅛ in) thick. Season with salt and pepper, and mix in the garlic. Grease a gratin dish with half the butter and arrange the potatoes in it.

Combine the milk and cream and pour over the potatoes. Shake the dish to distribute everything well and then sprinkle the gruyère on top. Dot with remaining butter and bake in the preheated oven for about 1 hour or until the potatoes are soft. Serve sprinkled with chopped parsley.

grilled vegetables

1 medium-sized eggplant

2 medium-sized zucchini

1 capsicum

1 medium-sized fennel bulb

200 g (about 7 oz) butternut pumpkin

6 tbsp olive oil

1 tsp finely chopped fresh rosemary

1 tsp finely chopped fresh lemon thyme

¼ tsp ground sweet paprika

salt and freshly ground black pepper

Easy to cook, delicious and always popular. Choose the most gorgeous-looking seasonal vegetables.

Wash eggplant and zucchini, then cut into 1 cm (½ in) slices. Cut capsicum lengthwise into 4 or 5 pieces, as flat as possible, remove seeds, and trim if necessary. Remove any damaged fennel leaves and cut the bulb lengthwise into 1 cm (½ in) slices.

Peel the pumpkin and cut into slices 1 cm (½ in) thick.

In a bowl, mix the olive oil with the rosemary, lemon thyme and paprika, and season with pepper. Brush the vegetables with this preparation.

Barbecue the vegetables over a medium heat for a few minutes on each side. (Some vegetables, such as zucchini, cook more quickly, so add them last.) Season with salt and serve.

porcini polenta

with tomato and gruyère

S E R V E S 4

20 g (about ²/₃ oz) dried porcini mushrooms

¹/₂–³/₄ cup lukewarm water

1 tbsp olive oil

20 g (about ²/₃ oz) butter

2 tbsp chopped parsley

salt and freshly ground black pepper

extra ¹/₂ tsp salt

600 ml cold water

150 g (about 5 oz) instant polenta

12 semi-dried olives, pitted and halved

1 cup Italian-style tomato sauce

100 g (about 3¹/₂ oz) grated gruyère cheese

Like pasta and risotto, polenta is a great gift from Italian cuisine. This one is delicious on its own—a perfect vegetarian dish—or as an accompaniment to roast chicken or veal, or barbecued lamb or quail.

Soak the mushrooms in the lukewarm water for 20 minutes. Strain, reserving the liquid, then wash the mushrooms in cold water. Drain, then cut the mushrooms into small pieces.

Heat the oil and half the butter in a frying pan and gently cook the mushrooms for 1 minute. Add the mushroom liquid and cook until it has almost all evaporated. Stir in parsley and season with salt and pepper. Turn the heat off.

Preheat oven to 220°C/450°F. In a saucepan, add the ¹/₂ teaspoon of salt to the cold water and bring to the boil on the stove. Slowly pour in the polenta, lower heat and stir until the polenta has thickened. Season with pepper. Stir in the olives, mushrooms and remaining butter (don't overmix, because the mushroom juices will give the polenta an unattractive colour). Pour the polenta into a buttered gratin dish and spread evenly. Bake in the preheated oven for 8 minutes.

Remove the polenta from the oven and spread it with the tomato sauce. Sprinkle with the gruyère and return to the oven until the cheese has melted and the top is lightly browned.

green flageolet bean casserole

with parsley

S ERVES 4

1½ cups dried green flageolet beans

3 cloves garlic

2 sprigs of thyme

50 g (almost 2 oz) butter

salt and freshly ground black pepper

4 tbsp chopped parsley

Green flageolet beans are one of my favourite legumes and one of the most delicate. In France they are often served with roast lamb or in salads. Although this recipe uses dried beans, you can substitute canned ones. You can also use other dried beans, such as haricot or cannellini.

Place the beans in a bowl, cover with cold water to come 5 cm (2 in) above the beans and soak in the fridge for at least 12 hours or overnight.

Drain the soaked beans and place in a saucepan with 2 of the garlic cloves and the thyme. (Don't add salt at this stage, as this toughens the beans.) Cover with cold water, bring to the boil and simmer for 40–60 minutes or until the beans are tender. Drain, discarding the garlic and herbs.

Heat the butter in a saucepan and gently toss the cooked beans in it. Season with salt and pepper, and add the parsley and remaining garlic clove (chopped).

Serve with your favourite bread, toasted perhaps.

mussels

with ginger and coriander

about 40 large mussels

2 shallots, finely sliced

2 tbsp dry white wine

freshly ground black pepper

1 tsp finely grated ginger root

1 tbsp soy sauce

½ clove garlic, finely chopped

juice of ½ lemon

1 tsp honey

½ small chilli, very finely sliced

¼ tsp sesame oil

1 tbsp peanut oil

2 tbsp chopped fresh coriander

The flavour combination and the texture of plump mussels are out of this world. Serve hot or cold, and select very fresh, large heavy mussels.

Clean the mussels well, rubbing the shells against each other in cold water to remove any sand trapped inside. Place them in a large saucepan with the shallots and wine. Season with pepper, cover the pan and cook over a high heat for a minute or two until the shells open. During this time, shake the pan to allow the mussels at the top to fall to the bottom. Drain the mussels and keep the juice for use later in a soup or sauce. Detach the mussels from the shells and place them on plates for serving. (You can also serve the mussels in a half shell if you like.)

In a small bowl, combine the ginger, soy sauce, garlic, lemon juice, honey, chilli, sesame oil, peanut oil and coriander. Spoon a little of this mixture over each mussel and serve immediately.

pan-fried ocean trout

with watercress sauce

SERVES 4

4 cups watercress, washed

4 ocean trout cutlets, each weighing about
150 g (about 5 oz)

a little plain flour

salt and freshly ground black pepper

2 tbsp olive oil

6 tbsp crème fraiche or sour cream

a few sprigs of extra watercress

4 lemon wedges

The contrast between the pink of the trout and the pale green of the watercress sauce is a delight to the eye.

Bring a saucepan of water to the boil. Add the watercress and boil for 3 minutes. Drain then blend to a purée.

Lightly coat the trout cutlets with flour and season with salt and pepper. Heat the oil in a non-stick pan and cook the cutlets for 2–3 minutes on each side.

Place the cream and watercress purée in a saucepan and boil for 1 minute to let the mixture blend and reduce a little. Spoon this sauce onto serving plates and top with the trout cutlets. Add a sprig of cress, and serve immediately with a wedge of lemon.

steamed whiting fillets
with a leek and mushroom sauce

100 g (about 3$\frac{1}{2}$ oz) butter, cut into small cubes

1 shallot or $\frac{1}{4}$ white onion, finely chopped

6 medium-sized mushrooms, finely sliced

1 cup very finely sliced leeks (about $\frac{1}{2}$ leek)

salt and freshly ground black pepper

$\frac{1}{3}$ cup dry white wine

8 whiting fillets, each weighing about 100 g (3$\frac{1}{2}$ oz)

a few sprigs of herbs (e.g. parsley, chervil) for garnish

A fine French fish dish which reminds me of my grandmother's cooking. It is well worthwhile opening a fine bottle of dry white wine to wash it down in the gentlest way.

Melt one or two cubes of butter in a large frying pan and stir in the shallot. Spread the mushrooms and leeks on top and season with salt and pepper. Add the wine, bring to the boil, cover with foil or a lid and cook over a medium heat for 5 minutes. Remove the lid and place the fish fillets on top of the vegetables, skin side down. Season with a little salt and pepper. Cover pan again and steam the fish over a medium heat for about 5 minutes or until the fish is just cooked.

Lift the fish and vegetables onto warm serving plates, leaving the cooking liquid in the pan. Bring this to the boil and reduce it quickly to 2 or 3 tablespoons. Whisk in the remaining butter until just melted. Season the sauce to taste and spoon over fish. Garnish with herbs, then serve.

baked snapper with white wine and herbs

S E R V E S   4

60 g (2 oz) butter

6 shallots, finely sliced

3 sprigs of lemon thyme or common thyme

4 sprigs of parsley

3–4 sprigs of dill or a sprig of tarragon

200 g (about 7 oz) button mushrooms

3 tomatoes, sliced

a 1.5 kg (about 3 lb) snapper

salt and freshly ground black pepper

1 cup dry white wine, e.g. chardonnay

A Mediterranean dish par excellence. Baking with wine is one of the easiest ways to cook a whole fish, and snapper is a great choice.

Preheat the oven to 200°C/400°F.

Use half the butter to grease a roasting tray or ovenproof dish large enough to hold the fish. (If size is a problem, cut off the fish tail.) Place shallots, thyme, parsley, dill, mushrooms and tomato in the dish. Lay the fish on top, having first seasoned it on both sides with salt and pepper. Pour white wine over, and dot with the remaining butter. Cover dish tightly with foil and bake in the preheated oven for about 25 minutes. Remove from oven and leave to stand for 5–10 minutes before serving (the fish will finish cooking during this time).

Serve fish from the centre of the table. (It is easier if one person portions it.)

pan-fried john dory with a chardonnay sauce

S E R V E S   4

100 g (about 3½ oz) butter

3 shallots or ½ medium-sized white onion, very finely chopped

⅓ cup chardonnay or other dry white wine

⅓ cup fish stock (page 166) or water

1 tbsp cream

2 tbsp vegetable oil

600 g (about 1¼ lb) John Dory fillets, cut into 4 pieces

salt and freshly ground black pepper

a few sprigs of chervil or parsley (optional)

The sauce of chardonnay and shallots is a variation on the classic beurre blanc (page 169). Buy whole fish and ask your fishmonger to fillet it for you.

Heat a small knob of the butter in a saucepan and stir-fry the shallots or onion for 1 minute without browning. Add the wine, bring to the boil and cook over a medium heat until almost evaporated. Add the stock and boil down until reduced by about half. Add the cream, bring to the boil, then put aside.

Meanwhile, heat oil in a large frying pan (use two pans if necessary) and cook the Dory fillets over a medium heat for 2–3 minutes on each side. Season with salt and pepper. When the fish is almost cooked, whisk the remaining butter into the sauce and season with salt and pepper. Place fish on plates, spoon sauce over and garnish with herbs.

yabbies

with a vegetable sauce

TO COOK THE YABBIES

3 litres (about 5½ pts) water

¾ cup dry white wine

1 white onion, cut into 8 segments

1 medium-sized carrot, sliced

1 clove

a bouquet garni of thyme, parsley and ½ bay leaf

a little sea salt

32 uncooked yabbies

TO ASSEMBLE THE DISH

1 kg (about 2 lb) ripe tomatoes

2 tbsp butter

1 white onion, finely chopped

1 medium-sized carrot, cut into 5 mm (¼ in) dice

1 stick of celery, cut into 5 mm (¼ in) dice

2 sprigs of lemon thyme

salt and freshly ground black pepper

2 tbsp cognac or brandy

a pinch of cayenne

2 cloves garlic, chopped

2 tbsp finely snipped chives

A freshly cooked, plump yabby is a great treat. Don't miss the opportunity if it arises.

Place all ingredients for the cooking liquid in a large saucepan. Bring to the boil and simmer for 10 minutes. Add the uncooked yabbies and return the liquid nearly to boiling point. Cook the yabbies, without boiling, for 4 minutes and then drain. (You can discard this liquid on your compost heap.)

Halve the tomatoes, squeeze out the seeds and chop the flesh coarsely. Melt half the butter in a saucepan and cook half the chopped onion with the carrot and celery for 5 minutes. Add the tomatoes and the thyme, season with salt and pepper, and cook for 10 minutes.

Meanwhile, shell the yabbies. Heat the remaining butter in a frying pan and cook the remaining onion for 3 minutes. Add the yabbies and stir to reheat. Add cognac or brandy and bring to the boil. Add the vegetable sauce and season with a pinch of cayenne and the garlic. Serve sprinkled with chives.

crayfish tartlets

with coriander

S E R V E S 4

200 g (about 7 oz) puff pastry (page 175)

1 tbsp Italian-style tomato sauce

$\frac{1}{2}$ cup finely sliced leeks

$\frac{1}{2}$ tbsp butter

1 tbsp very finely chopped carrots

1 tbsp very finely chopped celery

6 very white, medium-sized mushrooms, diced

sea salt and freshly ground black pepper

1 cooked crayfish, weighing around 1 kg (2 lb)

1 tbsp olive oil

1 tbsp very finely chopped fresh coriander

2 tsp lemon juice

$\frac{1}{8}$ tsp chilli paste

extra 2 tbsp chopped coriander for garnish

A dish of total indulgence: savour the contrast between crisp pastry and succulent slices of crayfish, and the subtle Asian seasonings.

Preheat the oven to 200°C/400°F.

Roll out the pastry to about 3 mm ($\frac{1}{8}$ in) thick, then cut out 4 rounds each 10 cm (4 in) in diameter. Place on an oven sheet and prick with a fork. In a small bowl, mix the tomato sauce with the sliced leeks. Spread a little of this mixture over each pastry round, leaving a 5 mm margin round the edge. Bake in the preheated oven until the base is lightly browned (this takes about 15 minutes).

Meanwhile, heat the butter in a small saucepan and cook the carrots and celery in it over a low heat for 5 minutes. Add the mushrooms and cook until soft. Season with salt and pepper.

Shell the crayfish and cut the tail into 3–4 mm (about $\frac{1}{8}$ in) slices. Keep the flesh from the legs for another use (perhaps a salad).

Mix the olive oil with the chopped coriander, the lemon juice and the chilli paste.

Place 1 tablespoon of the hot mushroom mixture onto each cooked pastry round. Arrange crayfish slices neatly on top and brush these with the oil and coriander dressing. Cook in the preheated oven for 2–3 minutes, just to reheat the crayfish. Serve immediately, garnished with chopped coriander.

prawn and leek salad

with a walnut dressing

24 medium-sized green king prawns (or other
large prawns)

12 baby leeks, about 1 cm ($\frac{1}{2}$ in) in diameter

200 g (about 7 oz) small French beans, topped
and tailed

1 shallot, finely chopped

$\frac{3}{4}$ tbsp red wine or raspberry vinegar

salt and freshly ground black pepper

2 tbsp walnut oil or olive oil

150 g (about 5 oz) mixed small leafy greens

2 tbsp finely chopped walnuts

2 tbsp finely snipped chives

A superb spring dish to be enjoyed with a very fine white wine. If possible, buy uncooked prawns. If baby leeks are unavailable, you could use asparagus or small leeks cut into 5 cm lengths.

Place the prawns in a large amount of boiling salted water. Allow the water to almost return to the boil and then cook the prawns for 1 minute. Drain, and plunge prawns briefly in cold water to cool and stop them cooking. Drain prawns, and shell and devein them.

Steam or boil the leeks and beans until just tender. Plunge into cold water to stop the cooking, then drain.

In a bowl, combine the chopped shallot with the red wine vinegar. Season with salt and pepper, and mix in the oil. Season the prawns with half this dressing, and the leeks and beans with the remainder.

Divide the green leaves between 4 plates. Top with the leeks and beans, then with the prawns. Sprinkle with chopped walnuts and chives and serve.

bouillabaisse

(a mediterranean fish soup)

2 kg (about 4 lb) mixed shellfish
and fish, cleaned

2 tbsp virgin olive oil

1 medium-sized onion, chopped

10 cumin seeds

20 fennel seeds

1 small hot chilli

1 fennel bulb, cut into 12 wedges, or 4 sticks
of celery, each cut into 3

1 kg (about 2lb) tomatoes, peeled, seeded and
flesh chopped coarsely

1 litre (about 2 pts) fish stock (page 166),
prawn stock (page 167) or vegetable
broth (page 167)

salt and freshly ground black pepper

a large pinch of saffron threads

12 small new potatoes, cooked

2 cloves garlic, chopped

Bouillabaisse is not a dish—it is a celebration of the sea. It is also a feast for the senses, with its fresh aroma, interesting textures and golden hue. The challenge lies in obtaining a good range of firm fish (such as gurnard, John Dory and flathead) and shellfish (such as crayfish and prawns). Bouillabaisse is traditionally served with croûtons and a rouille (page 171).

Cut fish and shellfish into 4 cm (1½–2 in) pieces, leaving the bones in.

Heat oil in a casserole dish over a gentle heat and fry the onion, cumin, fennel seeds and chilli for 1 minute. Add fennel wedges and fry for 1 minute before stirring in the tomatoes. Place fish and shellfish neatly on top and then pour stock over, adding a little water to cover the fish if necessary. Season with salt, pepper and saffron, then bring to the boil and simmer for 10 minutes.

Transfer fish and shellfish from the liquid to a large dish. (If you wish, you can remove the fish bones first.) Place potatoes around the edge. Add garlic to the cooking liquid and serve this in a soup tureen.

Everyone can help themselves to the fish and potatoes, then pour the hot soup over.

treats
for two

A tête-à-tête dinner with a loved one is a wonderful treat. Cooking for two usually takes less time than cooking for a group, and when buying for two even the most expensive foods seem quite affordable. These days, in order to enjoy more of each other's company, my wife and I try to keep food preparation and cooking to a minimum. We may cook one or two special dishes, and make a salad rather than cooking vegetables. For the rest, we often choose prepared foods from the huge range that is now available: antipasto ingredients, smoked salmon, sushi, pâtés and terrines, a Chinese roast duck, good cheeses and breads, and gourmet ice-creams, cakes and pastries. Shopkeepers are now making life easier for those cooking for one or two, with trimmed, easy-to-carve cuts of meat, manageable portions of poultry and fish, and wonderful seafood.

At home, we prepare our favourite soups and casseroles in sufficient quantity to last for two or three meals. Sometimes, too, we freeze freshly made dishes to have on hand when we don't feel like cooking. So the only part of the meal to which we need to devote a little more time is the selection of the champagne.

salad of scampi and asparagus

with truffle

SERVES 2

1 small truffle, weighing
about 20 g (^{2}/$_3$ oz)
2 tbsp olive oil
about 12 asparagus spears
1 shallot, very finely chopped
^{1}/$_2$ tbsp raspberry vinegar
salt and freshly ground black pepper
about 24 leaves of lamb's lettuce
or other greens
12 uncooked scampi, shelled and deveined
a few sprigs of chervil

Brush the truffle briefly under running water, then dry it with kitchen paper. Slice the truffle very thinly, put 4 slices aside and cut the remainder into thin strips. Place the strips and the slices in a small dish and cover with 1 tablespoon of the olive oil.

Wash asparagus and boil for about 3 minutes or until just tender. Drain, cool in ice-cold water, then drain again.

In a bowl, combine the shallot and vinegar with a little salt and pepper. Add the truffle and olive oil mixture, keeping the 4 slices aside for garnish. Place the lettuce and asparagus in a salad bowl and season with half of the dressing.

Heat the remaining oil in a non-stick frying pan and cook the scampi for about 30 seconds on each side. Divide the asparagus and lettuce between 2 plates and arrange the scampi around the edge. Spoon the remaining dressing over the scampi and place slices of truffle on top. Garnish with the chervil and serve.

prawn risotto

with preserved lemon

A risotto for special occasions, this takes just under an hour to prepare. The preserved lemon adds a touch of freshness: if you can't find any, use a teaspoon of lemon zest instead. Serve with a green salad and a fine riesling.

SERVES 2

12 large uncooked prawns

2 tbsp olive oil

10 fennel seeds

$^1\!/_3$ cup dry white wine

1 tsp tomato paste

2 sprigs of parsley

1 litre (about 2 pints) boiling water

salt and freshly ground black pepper

1 pinch of cayenne

$^1\!/_2$ medium-sized onion, finely chopped

150 g (about 5 oz) arborio rice (Italian round-grain rice)

1 cup cooked peas

about 30 g (1 oz) preserved lemon, diced

20 g (about $^2\!/_3$ oz) butter

1 tbsp freshly grated parmesan

a few sprigs of chervil or 1 tbsp chopped parsley

Shell and devein the prawns, and put them in the fridge. (Keep the shells for the stock.)

Heat 1 tablespoon of the oil in a medium-sized saucepan and stir-fry the prawn shells and fennel seeds over a high heat for 3–4 minutes. Add the wine and tomato paste and boil for 30 seconds. Add the parsley and water, season with salt, pepper and cayenne, and simmer for 20 minutes.

Strain the prawn shells, pressing on them to extract as much as possible of the flavoursome stock. Place the stock in a saucepan and bring to a simmer.

Heat the remaining oil in a medium-sized saucepan and gently fry the onion for 3 minutes. Add the rice and stir well for 1 minute. Add about one-third of the hot stock and stir gently over a low heat. When almost all the stock has been absorbed, add another half cupful and stir gently again. Continue adding stock a little at a time until the rice is cooked but still firm in the centre. (The whole process takes about 20 minutes.)

Five minutes before the rice is ready, cook the peas in boiling water. Place the prawns in the remainder of the hot stock and poach them for 30–60 seconds or until they change colour. Try a few grains of rice to see whether it's cooked: the risotto should be creamy but not runny. Now add to it the prawns, drained peas, preserved lemon, butter and parmesan, and mix gently. Turn off the heat, cover with a lid and allow to rest for 3 minutes. Before serving, garnish with the chervil or parsley.

grilled crayfish

with fines herbes

20 g (about 2/3 oz) butter

2 tbsp olive oil

salt and freshly ground black pepper

1 pinch of cayenne

1 small clove garlic, very finely chopped

1 tsp finely chopped fresh lemon thyme

1 tbsp finely chopped tarragon

1 tbsp finely chopped parsley

1 tsp brandy

an 800 g (about 1 3/4 lb) uncooked crayfish

3 tbsp fresh breadcrumbs

I adore crayfish! Here, it is just lightly grilled and still moist, with a soupçon of herbs and a light crust of breadcrumbs. I have simple tastes . . .

Preheat the griller to medium.

Melt the butter and oil in a small saucepan, turn off the heat and season with salt, pepper and cayenne. Stir in the garlic, lemon thyme, tarragon, parsley and brandy.

Cut the crayfish in half lengthwise and remove the intestines. Place, cut side up, in an oven dish just large enough to hold both halves. Brush the flesh with the seasoned butter and oil, and sprinkle with breadcrumbs, patting them down slightly.

Position the dish so the crayfish is about 8 cm (about 3 in) from the grill and cook for 10–15 minutes. (Keep an eye on it and make sure it does not burn.) Alternatively, you can cook it in a very hot oven (250°C/500°F), also for 10–15 minutes.

pan-fried red mullet
with anchovy and basil butter

Serves 2

4 red mullet, each weighing 120 g (4 oz)

4 anchovy fillets

60 g (2 oz) butter, cut into cubes

juice of $\frac{1}{2}$ lemon

3 fresh basil leaves

freshly ground black pepper

a little plain flour

salt and freshly ground black pepper

2 tbsp olive oil

extra $\frac{1}{2}$ lemon for squeezing

Fragile but so flavoursome, red mullet is beloved of Europeans and my own favourite fish. It must be extremely fresh.

Have the fish scaled and cleaned, but leave them whole.

Place the anchovy fillets, about two-thirds of the butter, the lemon juice, basil leaves and a little pepper in a food processor and blend until well combined. Transfer to a small sheet of foil and shape the mixture into a cylinder about 3 cm in diameter. Refrigerate until it is firm (if you are short of time, put it in the freezer).

Dry the fish and coat well with flour which you have seasoned with some salt and pepper. Heat the oil in a frying pan and cook the fish on one side for 3 minutes. Turn them over, add remaining butter to pan and cook for a further 2–3 minutes.

Slice the anchovy butter into 4. Divide the fish between two warmed plates, squeeze a little lemon juice over and garnish each fish with a slice of anchovy butter. Serve with a salad of curly endive.

crayfish in broth

with a vegetable julienne

A perfect dish for a romantic dinner.
You can prepare it in advance and
reheat it at the last minute.

SERVES 2

6 cups water

1 cup dry white wine, e.g. chardonnay

a bouquet garni (thyme, parsley
and $^1/_2$ bay leaf)

1 small onion, pierced with a clove

2 sticks of celery

2 medium-sized carrots

salt and freshly ground black pepper

an uncooked crayfish weighing 600–800 g
(about $1^1/_4$–$1^3/_4$ lb)

1 egg white

6 coriander seeds, crushed (optional)

a pinch of cayenne

25 fresh coriander leaves

In a saucepan large enough to hold the crayfish, place the water, wine, bouquet garni and the onion. Thinly slice 1 celery stick and 1 carrot and add these too. Season with salt and pepper, bring to the boil and cook for 10 minutes. Now add the crayfish to the pan and simmer for a further 15 minutes (do not let it boil, or the crayfish will toughen).

Transfer the crayfish to a plate and strain the cooking liquid into a clean pan. Bring the liquid back to the boil, whisk in the egg white and simmer for 5 minutes: the egg white will coagulate and absorb any impurities from the broth. Strain the broth using a very fine sieve or a damp cloth over a strainer.

Cut the remaining carrot and celery into julienne (very fine sticks about 6 cm long and 1 mm thick). Add these to the liquid with the coriander seeds and cayenne, and simmer for 2 minutes.

Shell the crayfish and remove the flesh from the legs and head. Cut the tail into bite-sized pieces. Season flesh with salt and pepper, then reheat in the hot broth and vegetables for 10–20 seconds. Serve in two deep soup bowls and sprinkle with coriander leaves.

warm oysters

in a champagne sauce

A romantic dish for those who believe that living on love is not enough. You also need oysters and champagne!

SERVES 2

18 freshly opened oysters, in their shells

1 shallot, very finely chopped

1 tbsp red wine vinegar

4 tbsp champagne or sparkling wine

1 tsp whipping cream

30 g (about 1 oz) butter, cut into small cubes

salt and freshly ground black pepper

2 tsp finely snipped chives

Preheat the oven to warm (100°C/210°F). Remove the oysters from their shells and place in a bowl. Wash the shells, place on an oven tray and put in the warm oven.

In a small saucepan over a low heat, cook the chopped shallot in the vinegar and half the champagne until the liquid has almost all evaporated. Stir in the cream and then whisk in the butter. Season with salt and pepper, and put aside.

Pour the remaining champagne into a small pan and bring to the boil. Add the oysters, shake the pan to distribute the heat and leave for 20 seconds (but don't let it boil). Remove the oysters, drain, and place them in the warm shells. Spoon a little hot sauce over each oyster and season with some extra pepper. Sprinkle with chives and serve immediately.

fish cutlet masala

SERVES 2

2 tsp ground cumin

1 tsp ground turmeric

2 tsp finely grated ginger root

$\frac{1}{4}$ tsp salt

1 tbsp garam masala

2 fish cutlets each weighing 150 g (about 5 oz), or 1 large cutlet

2 tbsp rice flour

2 tbsp vegetable oil

A spice tour of tropical southern India led me to a great seafood restaurant on the beach outside Madras where I was introduced to simple Indian fish cookery. For this dish the spices must be fresh and the fish even fresher.

On a plate mix together the cumin, turmeric, ginger, salt and garam masala. Rub this spicy mixture all over the fish cutlets, cover with plastic wrap or foil and refrigerate for about 30 minutes.

Put the rice flour on a plate and lightly flour the fish. Heat oil in a non-stick frying pan and cook the fish for 2½–3 minutes on each side. Serve with rice, chutney and Indian bread.

scallops

with a leek and walnut purée

A delicate yet rich dish best served with slices of fresh baguette to soak up the delicious sauce. And with a glass of Alsace riesling.

SERVES 2

1 medium-sized leek

20 g (about ²⁄₃ oz) butter

3 tbsp water

salt and freshly ground black pepper

2 tbsp dry vermouth

½ cup strong fish stock (page 166)

250 g (about 9 oz) very fresh scallops, well-cleaned

3 tbsp cream

1 tbsp very finely chopped walnuts

6 sprigs of chervil

Remove any damaged leek leaves. Trim off the top part, leaving about 5 cm (2 in) of green. Cut leek in four lengthwise, leaving the root intact, wash well and then slice finely.

Heat butter over a medium heat and stir-fry the leek for about 4 minutes. Add the water and cook, covered, for about 10 minutes until the leek is soft. Blend to a fine purée and season with salt and pepper. Keep warm in a small pan.

Place the vermouth in a small saucepan, bring to the boil and reduce by half. Add the fish stock and bring to a simmer. Add the scallops and shake the pan to make sure they are all covered by the liquid. Cover the pan with foil and poach the scallops for about 30 seconds, until they just whiten. Remove scallops, then return the cooking liquid to a quick boil and reduce by half. Add the cream, bring to the boil again and reduce briefly to a sauce consistency. Return the scallops to the pan, stir so that they are all coated with the sauce, then season to taste.

Add the walnuts to the leek purée and divide this mixture between two hot plates, spreading it a little. Spoon scallops and sauce on top, and serve garnished with the chervil.

THE PLEASURE OF WINE

I WAS ONLY FIVE OR SIX BUT IT SEEMS LIKE ONLY YESTERDAY WHEN MY father invited me to help him make wine for the very first time. It was a proud moment. The family wine press consisted of a several hundred kilogram antique affair that had been pressing the Gaté grapes for many generations. The contraption stood on large wooden and iron wheels which allowed it to be hauled all over the village from one family member's cellar to another. The harvest season was sacred and every hand, young and old, was required to ensure there was good wine on the table for the year to come. Apart from what he had inherited from his parents, my father planted one hundred vines each time one of us was born, to guarantee that production would meet future consumption. We always had more than sufficient wine and the excess was exchanged with neighbours and friends for other goods, such as wood and compost, a turkey at Christmas, wild rabbits and hare during the hunting season, walnuts and hazelnuts in autumn.

Wine is one of the great pleasures of life. As Max Lake, the respected Australian surgeon, writer and winemaker once said, 'The appreciation of wine itself is truly a very simple matter. It must look good, smell good and taste good.'

Because wine is a liquid, our tastebuds can easily register its flavours. Whether white, red or rosé, a good wine exhibits a complex flavour of fruit and other plants. Wine writers often describe wines that taste like lime, peach, passionfruit, quince, raspberries, cherries, plums, licorice, vanilla and chocolate, just to mention a few. I have found it of great benefit to join a wine appreciation course to learn about and understand this wonderful substance. The secret to matching food and wine is to find a common flavour element between the two, and this takes a little experience. Ultimately, the idea is to enjoy wine with food and other people. And if the blend is not perfect, who cares!

WALTER'S WINE BAR
This Pinot Noir was
especially blended by
Walter Bourke & Phillip Jones
at Bass Phillip Winery
• 1993 Vintage •
Bourgogne

spaghetti

with prawns and pernod

S ERVES 2

500 g (about 1 lb) green prawns

2 tbsp olive oil

$^{1}/_{2}$ medium-sized brown onion, finely sliced

10 fennel seeds

3 sprigs of lemon thyme

2 tbsp dry white wine

1 tsp tomato paste

500 g (about 1 lb) ripe tomatoes, chopped

salt and freshly ground black pepper

1 pinch of cayenne

200 g (about 7 oz) spaghetti

$^{1}/_{2}$ tbsp butter

1 small stick of celery, finely diced

1 small carrot, finely diced

2 tsp Pernod

1 clove garlic, finely chopped

1 tbsp chopped parsley

A fine, spicy dish. You can prepare the sauce and cook the spaghetti several hours in advance: if so, cool the pasta straight away in iced water, then drain it and toss in a little olive oil. Refrigerate until needed, and reheat in simmering water for a minute when you need it.

Shell and devein the prawns (keep the shells for making the sauce). Refrigerate the prawn meat immediately.

Put the oil in a large saucepan over a high heat. Add the prawn shells, onion, fennel seeds and lemon thyme, and stir for 5 minutes. Add the wine and boil for 30 seconds. Add tomato paste and chopped tomatoes, and season with salt, pepper and cayenne. Cover and cook over a medium heat for 20 minutes. Strain the sauce, pressing the prawn shells to extract their juice.

Meanwhile, cook the spaghetti in a large amount of salted boiling water till al dente.

Heat the butter in a large frying pan over a medium heat. Add the celery and carrot, and cook for 3 minutes. Add prawns and stir-fry until they change colour. Add the Pernod, bring to the boil and add the prepared sauce. Bring to a simmer, stir in the garlic and parsley, and season to taste. Toss with the drained spaghetti, then serve.

salad of fresh and smoked salmon

S E R V E S   2

a 200 g (about 7 oz) piece of fresh Atlantic
salmon, skin left on

1 tbsp olive oil

salt and freshly ground black pepper

½ butter lettuce

100 g (about 3½ oz) smoked salmon

1 hard-boiled egg, shelled and sliced

6 cherry tomatoes

1 tbsp salmon roe

1 tbsp finely snipped chives

juice of ½ lemon

3 tbsp runny cream

1 tsp hot mustard (optional)

1 tbsp finely chopped fresh dill

Double salmon pleasure. A summer dish that cries out for a glass of pink champagne and some good, crusty bread.

Preheat the oven to 150°C/300°F.

Brush the fresh salmon with olive oil and season with salt and pepper. Place on a small oven tray, skin-side up, and bake in the preheated oven for about 15 minutes. Remove from oven and leave to cool.

Wash and dry the lettuce leaves and use them to line a serving platter. Skin the cooked salmon, flake the flesh using your fingers, and scatter the flakes over the lettuce. Place small slices of smoked salmon, the egg slices and the cherry tomatoes on top. Sprinkle with the salmon roe and half the chives.

Mix lemon juice, cream and mustard in a bowl, and season with salt and pepper. Stir in the dill and the remaining chives. Serve this dressing separately.

brussels sprout and parsley purée

S E R V E S   2

800 g (about 1¾ lb) brussels sprouts

⅔ cup milk

½ cup parsley leaves

20 g (about ⅔ oz) butter

salt and freshly ground black pepper

The smoothness and rich flavour of this purée never fails to surprise. Most people find it hard to believe that its main ingredient is the humble brussels sprout.

Halve the sprouts, removing any damaged outer leaves, and wash well in cold water. Steam or boil for about 10 minutes or until tender, then drain.

Bring the milk and parsley to the boil, then remove from the heat. Blend the sprouts, milk, parsley and butter to a purée. Season with salt and pepper, then serve.

If making the purée in advance, reheat it in the microwave or in the oven at a very low temperature, stirring frequently.

fettuccine with smoked salmon and asparagus

Spring indulgence: a dish of al dente pasta served with tender asparagus and mouthwatering, salty salmon.

SERVES 2

20 thin asparagus tips, about 6 cm (2½ in) long

150 g (about 5 oz) fresh fettuccine

20 g (about ⅔ oz) butter

¼ medium-sized white onion, finely chopped

½ cup chicken stock (page 165)

2 tbsp crème fraîche or sour cream

salt and freshly ground black pepper

1 tbsp freshly grated parmesan

100 g (about 3½ oz) smoked salmon, cut into fine strips

a few sprigs of chervil

Bring a large saucepan of salted water to the boil and cook the asparagus tips for 1 minute. Remove from pan with a slotted spoon.

Cook the pasta in boiling salted water until al dente. Meanwhile, heat the butter in a frying pan and cook the onion for 2 minutes. Add the asparagus and stir for 30 seconds. Add the stock, bring to the boil and then reduce until only a couple of tablespoonsful of stock remain. Add the crème fraîche, bring to the boil, season with salt and pepper, and stir in the parmesan. Gently toss this mixture through the pasta and serve garnished with the smoked salmon and chervil.

fusilli with a puttanesca sauce

A quick but very tasty dish for a busy weekend. The sauce, scattered with morsels of olives, anchovies and herbs, is sharp and coats the curly pasta beautifully.

SERVES 2

200 g (about 7 oz) long fusilli

1½ tbsp olive oil

1 clove garlic, finely chopped

2 anchovy fillets, cut into small pieces

200 g (about 7 oz) canned peeled tomatoes, chopped

6 black olives, pitted and cut into long pieces

1 tsp finely chopped fresh oregano or basil, or ½ tsp dried oregano

1 tbsp chopped parsley

salt and freshly ground black pepper

2 tbsp freshly grated parmesan

Bring a large pan of salted water to the boil and cook the pasta until al dente.

Meanwhile, heat the oil in a non-stick frying pan over a medium heat. Stir in the garlic and anchovies for 10 seconds, then increase the heat and add the tomatoes and olives. Bring to the boil and stir for 2 minutes. Add the oregano and parsley, and season to taste with salt and pepper. Add the cooked pasta and toss together gently. Divide between 2 plates, and serve sprinkled with parmesan.

roast spatchcock
with lemon and herb stuffing

2 tbsp olive oil

½ medium-sized brown onion, finely chopped

1 tsp finely grated lemon zest

1 cup fresh breadcrumbs

1 tbsp finely chopped fresh tarragon or basil

1 tbsp finely chopped parsley

1 small egg, lightly beaten

salt and freshly ground black pepper

10 g (about ⅓ oz) butter, cut into small pieces

a 700 g (about 1½ lb) spatchcock

1 tsp finely chopped fresh lemon thyme

1 tbsp brandy or 3 tbsp dry white wine

1 cup strong chicken stock (page 165)

2 tsp cornflour mixed with 1 tbsp cold water

The herb and lemon stuffing gives the spatchcock (sometimes called 'poussin') extra class. If you wish you can use two 400 g (about 12 oz) birds rather than one larger one.

Preheat the oven to 180°C/350°F.

Heat half the oil in a small saucepan and gently fry the onion and lemon zest for 3 minutes. Place in a bowl and combine with the breadcrumbs, half the tarragon, the parsley, egg, a little salt and pepper and the butter. Spoon this stuffing into the cavity of the spatchcock, then truss the legs and wings with string. Brush bird with the remaining oil and the lemon thyme, and bake in the preheated oven for 15 minutes on each side.

Remove bird from oven, place on a plate, cover with foil and leave to rest while you make the sauce.

Add the brandy or wine to the pan and bring to the boil. Add stock and return to the boil. Whisk in the diluted cornflour to thicken the sauce and simmer for 3 minutes. Season with salt and pepper and stir in the remaining tarragon.

Halve the spatchcock and present each serve on a purée of brussels sprouts and parsley (page 87) with the stuffing and sauce spooned over the top. Roast potatoes are a good accompaniment.

EXCLUSIVE BUFFALO MILK
FARMERS CHEESE
(LIKE RICOT
from m
from those Victori
& made at M

THE FINE

grocer

When I was nineteen and had just finished my chef's apprenticeship, I ventured into the food department of Harrods in London and into Fauchon, the fine Parisian grocer. I was amazed at what I saw. I had already been thrilled by fresh produce markets, farms and groceries, but never before had I experienced the high of strolling through a large, eclectic and international food hall. I couldn't wait to try all the unfamiliar spices and seasonings, and to taste the foreign cheeses and exotic products spread before me. My visit to those two gastronomic temples opened up new horizons and made me realise that my career as a chef would take me to many distant and special places.

Now, years later, I still go to food halls and specialist grocery stores for inspiration and I almost always come away with some new ideas and products. Often such places stock things that are not available in supermarkets, like finer olive oils and foods prepared by artisans. One of my favourite grocers sells exceptional flageolets, haricots and other legumes, all kinds of condiments, including baby cornichons and capers, and good-quality powdered stocks. It also stocks the finest cooking chocolate, vanilla beans, coffee extract and flavoured syrups for use in making desserts.

Like other dedicated professionals, a good grocer is keen to please. Don't hesitate to ask for what you need and to explain what you need it for. Be adventurous. Try something you have never had before. The rewards are invaluable.

pepper steak

SERVES 2

2 well-trimmed steaks (e.g. fillet, sirloin, rump,
Scotch fillet)
1 tsp crushed black peppercorns, or
2 tsp crushed green peppercorns
1 tsp oil
1 tsp butter
salt
1/4 cup dry white wine
1/2 cup beef stock (page 164)
4 tbsp cream

Treat yourself and use fillet, sirloin, rump or Scotch fillet—the most tender cuts of beef. The sauce goes well with green vegetables such as French beans or spinach.

Sprinkle both sides of each steak with the peppercorns, pressing them in lightly with the palm of your hand.

Heat the oil and butter in a frying pan then add the steaks. Cook on one side for 2–4 minutes, depending on how you like your steak, then turn them over and cook the second side for another 2–4 minutes. Season the meat with salt, transfer to hot plates and cover with foil to keep warm while you make the sauce.

Add the wine to pan and bring to the boil. Add stock and boil over a high heat until reduced to about 3 tablespoons. Add the cream, and boil for a further minute. Season the sauce to taste with salt, pour over the steaks and serve immediately.

pan-fried loin of lamb with herbs and garlic

SERVES 2

2 pieces of lamb loin, each weighing
150 g (about 5 oz)
1 tbsp olive oil
2 tsp finely chopped fresh thyme
2 tsp finely chopped fresh rosemary
1 clove garlic, finely chopped
1/2 tsp finely crushed black pepper
salt

Sweet, tender, juicy, easy to cook and even easier to eat, especially if you use spring lamb. We harvest the thyme and rosemary from our garden—pure heaven.

Trim the lamb of fat and skin. In a bowl mix half the olive oil with the thyme, rosemary, garlic and black pepper. Rub the lamb with this seasoning and, if you have time, cover meat with plastic wrap and refrigerate for a couple of hours.

Heat the remaining oil in a non-stick pan and cook the meat for about 4–5 minutes on each side. Season with salt, then cover the meat with foil and rest it for 3–4 minutes before serving. A vegetable purée would go beautifully with it.

stir-fry of shiitake mushrooms

with chinese cabbage and bean sprouts

SERVES 2

200 g (about 7 oz) Chinese cabbage

100 g (about 3½ oz) fresh shiitake mushrooms

1 tbsp vegetable oil

2 tsp grated ginger root

½ clove garlic, crushed

100 g (about 3½ oz) bean sprouts

½ tbsp light soy sauce

¼ tsp sesame oil

¼ tsp chilli paste

2 spring onions, sliced

a few sprigs of coriander

The Chinese love shiitake mushrooms, which are a highlight in many of their dishes. For this stir-fry you can pre-boil the harder vegetables like beans and broccoli for 1–2 minutes before adding them to the wok. Make a quick feast of it by buying some Chinese roast pork, duck or chicken from a good take-away.

Wash the cabbage and slice it finely. Rinse the mushrooms and cut each into several pieces.

Heat the wok and add the vegetable oil. Stir in the ginger and garlic, then add the cabbage immediately. Stir-fry for 30 seconds then add the mushrooms. (If the cabbage starts sticking or burning, pour about a tablespoon of cold water down the side of the wok.) Cook until the cabbage and mushrooms have softened, then stir in the bean sprouts, soy sauce, sesame oil and chilli paste. Continue stirring until all the vegetables are just soft.

Serve garnished with the spring onions and coriander.

family
favourites

Each family has its own favourite dishes that everyone looks forward to sharing. Our children often clamour for a roast chicken, and in turn I sometimes long for some of my mother's and grandmother's special recipes from my childhood. Every cook stamps a dish with his or her own unique touch.

Sometimes we love a dish not so much for its flavour but because we associate it with a particular occasion, place or season. My favourite family dishes are mostly European in style and, like myself, of French origin. They are dishes of hearty flavours, like stews, soups and roasts. Dishes to be placed in the centre of the table for everyone to share and perhaps help themselves to another serving. Dishes to eat with bread and a green salad, and to be enjoyed with good wines.

Perhaps more than any other recipes, it's the family favourites that need to be recorded so that they can be passed on from one generation to the next. The easiest way to do this is to write down the recipe as you prepare it: be precise about ingredients and quantities ('half a cup of plain flour', 'a large carrot cut into 1 cm slices', and so on), and describe the method step by step. You can also add practical comments like 'This is best cooked in a non-stick pan' or 'Superb eaten the next day'. Collect all these recipes and let your family know that they are there.

minestrone

with rosemary

2 tbsp olive oil

2 cloves garlic, chopped

1 small brown onion, thinly sliced

$^1/_2$ tbsp chopped fresh rosemary

2 sticks of celery, diced

1 large carrot, diced

100 g (about 3$^1/_2$ oz) bacon, chopped

2 tbsp tomato paste, diluted in a
little hot water

$^1/_4$ cabbage, finely shredded

1 medium-sized leek, finely sliced

2 zucchini, diced

3 tbsp chopped parsley

1 clove

salt and freshly ground black pepper

1$^1/_2$ cups cooked beans, e.g. cannellini,
butter beans

2 tbsp finely grated parmesan

A meal on its own, which keeps well for two or three days. You don't need to worry too much about the way you cut the vegetables. You can use canned beans or cook your own.

Heat the olive oil in a large saucepan. Over a medium heat, add the garlic, onion, rosemary, celery, carrot and bacon and stir for about 5 minutes. Stir in the tomato paste and add the cabbage, leek, zucchinis, parsley and clove. Cover with hot water and season with salt and pepper. Bring to the boil and simmer for 20 minutes.

Meanwhile, drain the beans and blend half of them to a purée. Add the whole and puréed beans to the soup and simmer for a further 10 minutes. Sprinkle with parmesan before serving.

tomato and vegetable soup

SERVES 6

2 tbsp olive oil

½ large brown onion, diced

1 medium-sized carrot, diced

1 stick of celery, diced

2 sprigs of thyme

1 tbsp plain flour

1.5 kg (about 3 lb) tomatoes

4 cups chicken stock (page 165)

1 tsp sea salt

freshly ground black pepper

a pinch of cayenne

2 tbsp chopped parsley

1 clove garlic, chopped

1 tbsp butter

Texture is important in a good soup. I like to pass this one through a mouli: it produces a slightly coarse texture, which I prefer.

Heat the oil in a large saucepan and cook the onion, carrot, celery and thyme over a medium heat for 5 minutes. Stir in flour and make sure it is well combined. Add the tomatoes and stock, and season with salt, pepper and cayenne. Bring to the boil and simmer for 20 minutes.

Pass the soup through a mouli. (For a perfectly smooth texture, purée it in the blender and then strain it through a sieve.) Just before serving, season to taste and stir in the parsley, garlic and butter.

vegetable and potato soup

SERVES 6

1 red capsicum

1 stick of celery

1 medium-sized leek

2 medium carrots

1 tbsp olive oil or butter

2 medium-sized potatoes, peeled and diced

1 cup diced pumpkin

8 cups chicken stock (page 165) or water

salt and freshly ground black pepper

3 tbsp chopped parsley

A heart-warming and satisfying winter soup with stunning colour and texture. It can be prepared in next to no time and if you make a big pot it can be enjoyed over several days.

Wash and halve the capsicum. Remove the seeds and chop the flesh coarsely. Wash and then chop the celery and leek. Peel the carrots and chop them coarsely also.

Heat the oil or butter in a saucepan over a medium heat. Add the capsicum, celery, leek and carrots, and cook for about 5 minutes. Now add the potatoes, pumpkin and the stock. Bring to the boil, season with salt and pepper, and cook until all vegetables are tender. Stir in the parsley just before serving.

THE BUTCHER

RARE ARE THE WEEKENDS AT OUR PLACE WHEN WE DON'T PREPARE A special meat or poultry dish. In winter we have seasonal favourites such as a roast lamb or free-range chicken, or perhaps a veal stew simmered on top of the stove, mellow and warm. In the milder months we enjoy cooking small cuts on the barbecue, or pan-frying them to be served with a delicious sauce.

Finding a good butcher is not easy. A good butcher is friendly, takes the time to listen to your needs and tries to help you. A good butcher displays the meat neatly: I always check to make sure that the meat has been well trimmed of excess fat, gristle and bones (which are of no use to the cook), and that the chops and sliced meat have been cut uniformly (which is important for even cooking). I also look to see if the meat is bright and the fat white.

Unless committed to a recipe, I don't usually plan what to buy before I see what's on offer that day. There may be some superb spring lamb, young and tender veal, or aged rump for grilling. An excellent butcher understands how to cook meat and can advise about the best cuts for particular cooking methods. (My butcher in France even used to sell wines to serve with certain dishes.)

At the poultry shop the sale of free-range chickens, ducks and eggs is a good sign. A quality bird has plump breasts and strong-looking legs, and the shopkeeper will be happy to portion, skin or debone your poultry for you. Be daring and try something new, like pheasant, guinea fowl, squab or quail. It may become one of your specialties.

crème of cannellini

with leeks and peas

Hearty and yet delicately smooth. This soup really satisfies, especially when it is eaten, in the European tradition, with crusty bread.

SERVES 6–8

1.5 kg (about 3 lb) fresh cannellini beans or 2 cups dried cannellini beans

1 small leek

500 g (about 1 lb) unshelled peas

1 tbsp butter

4 cups vegetable (167) or chicken stock (page 165) or water

2 tbsp cream

about 20 sprigs of chervil or 3 tbsp finely snipped chives

If you are using dried beans, soak them in cold water for 12 hours before cooking. Shell the beans and place them in a saucepan of cold water. Bring to the boil and cook, without salt, for 30 minutes. Drain.

Meanwhile, wash and finely slice the leek and shell the peas. Heat the butter in a saucepan over a medium heat. Add the leek and stir for 3 minutes, then add the drained beans, cover with stock or water and boil for 20 minutes. Add the peas and cook for a further 10 minutes. Blend everything to a fine purée. Season with salt and pepper, and add boiling water if the soup is too thick.

Stir in the cream and serve sprinkled with chervil or chives, or both.

soup of chicken wings

and vegetables

A hearty, chunky soup which is one of my all-time favourites. The best chicken cut to use is winglets, which are tender and flavoursome.

SERVES 6

1 kg (about 2 lb) chicken winglets

3 litres (about 5½ pts) water

6 medium-sized carrots, peeled but left whole

1 medium-sized leek, washed and cut into 3 cm (1½ in) lengths

2 sticks of celery, cut into 3 cm (1½ in) lengths

a 5 mm (¼ in) slice of ginger root

1 clove

1 tsp sea salt

10 black peppercorns, crushed

6 spring onions

¼ cup fresh coriander leaves

Trim the chicken wings of as much fat as possible. Place them in a large saucepan and cover with the water. Add the carrots, the leek and celery pieces, the ginger and the clove, and season with salt and pepper. Bring to the boil and simmer for 30 minutes. After this time, remove the carrots, slice them and return them to the soup. If you wish, you can remove the bones from the chicken winglets.

When the soup is ready, slice the spring onion into small pieces and chop the coriander leaves finely. Serve the soup in bowls, with this garnish on top.

lamb curry

with fennel and peas

SERVES 6

3 cloves garlic

a 5 cm (2 in) piece of ginger root

1 small brown onion

2 tbsp vegetable oil

½ tsp cumin seeds

½ tsp fennel seeds

1 clove

2 cardamom pods

2 tbsp mild curry powder

1.2 kg (about 2½ lb) cubed lamb from the neck, shoulder or leg

6 medium-sized tomatoes, diced

salt and freshly ground black pepper

2 medium-sized fennel bulbs

1 cup boiling water

1 kg (about 2 lb) peas, shelled

1 tsp ground cumin

a handful of coriander leaves

For those who enjoy aromatic Indian food. The fennel adds softness and a subtle anise flavour. If you make the curry in advance, reheat it slowly and add a teaspoon of ground cumin just before serving, to lift the flavour.

Preheat oven to 150°C/300°F.

Crush the garlic, ginger and onion to a paste in a blender. Or chop them finely.

Heat the oil in an ovenproof casserole. Add the cumin and fennel seeds, the clove and the cardamom, and stir for 30 seconds. Add the onion paste, stir for 3 minutes, then add curry powder and stir well for a further minute. Increase the heat, add the lamb cubes and stir until the meat is well coated with the spices. Now add the tomatoes and stir well. Season with salt and pepper, cover with a lid and cook in the preheated oven for 1 hour.

Meanwhile, trim any damaged fennel leaves and cut each bulb into 8 segments. Add to the curry with the boiling water and stir well. Cover and cook for 45–60 minutes or until the lamb is tender. When it is almost cooked, cook the peas in a pot of boiling water for 5 minutes. Drain and add them to the curry with the ground cumin. Cook for a further 5 minutes and sprinkle the curry with coriander leaves before serving it with basmati rice.

roast shoulder of lamb

Serves 4–6

1 boned shoulder of spring lamb,
rolled and tied

2 cloves garlic, each cut into 6 long pieces

4 tbsp olive oil

1 tbsp finely chopped fresh thyme

$1/4$ tsp chilli paste

1 tsp freshly ground black pepper

2 or 3 sprigs of rosemary

1 onion, coarsely diced

1 carrot, coarsely diced

2 tbsp dry white wine

300 ml (about $1/2$ pt) veal stock (page 164)
or water

2 tsp cornflour mixed with 1 tbsp water

$1/2$ tsp sea salt

This dish spells Sunday lunch with the family. The shoulder makes the most flavoursome roast and is particularly tender and delicious when cooked as follows.

Preheat the oven to 220°C/450°F.

Using the tip of a sharp paring knife, make 12 small cuts in the lamb, between the strings. Insert the pieces of garlic into the holes.

Mix the olive oil, thyme, chilli paste and pepper in a bowl, then rub the lamb all over with this paste. Use kitchen string to tie the rosemary sprigs around the meat, then place it on an oven rack resting in a roasting tray. Roast for about 15 minutes, then turn the meat and add the onion and carrot. Lower the temperature to 160°C/320°F and roast for a further 30–50 minutes. Turn the meat once or twice more during this time, and baste it if there is enough fat.

Remove meat from the oven and place on a dish. Cover with foil and return to the oven at 80°C/170°F, with the door left slightly ajar, to rest for 10–15 minutes.

Meanwhile, drain as much fat as possible from the roasting tray, leaving in the onion and carrot. Place over a medium heat on top of the stove and add the wine, bring to the boil and reduce by half. Add the stock, return to the boil, whisk in the cornflour mixture and boil for 2 minutes. Strain into a small saucepan, season with salt and pepper, and keep warm on low heat.

After the lamb has rested, cut the strings and carve the meat into thin slices: it should be pink and tender. You can serve the sauce separately or spooned over the meat.

beef stroganoff

S ERVES 2

2 tbsp vegetable oil or butter

400 g (about 14 oz) button mushrooms, sliced

500 g (about 1 lb) beef fillet, cut into strips

2 tbsp sweet paprika

a pinch of cayenne

4 tbsp dry white wine

8 tbsp sour cream

salt and freshly ground black pepper

Tender meat coated with a rich and creamy spiced sauce. Stroganoff is a dream for the cook who loves hearty flavours but has little time to spend in the kitchen. Serve it with plain rice, pasta or mashed potato.

Heat half the oil in a non-stick frying pan or wok and cook the mushrooms over a high heat until soft. Transfer mushrooms to a plate, add remaining oil to the pan and stir-fry beef over a high heat until browned all over (but don't overcook it). Stir in the paprika and cayenne, then transfer the beef to the plate with the mushrooms.

Add the wine to pan and boil for 1 minute. Now add the cream and boil for 1 minute. Stir the mushrooms and beef into the sauce and reheat briefly. Season with salt and pepper and serve.

beef casserole

in shiraz

SERVES 6

12 pieces of oyster blade steak, each weighing
80–100 g (about 3–3$^{1}/_{2}$ oz)

1 medium-sized brown onion, sliced

2 sprigs of thyme

1 small bay leaf

6 sprigs of parsley

2 cloves garlic, crushed

1 clove

1 kg (about 2 lb) carrots, cut into 1 cm rounds

2 cups good shiraz

1 tbsp brandy or cognac

freshly ground black pepper

1 tbsp vegetable oil

1 tbsp butter

200 g (about 7 oz) bacon, cut into pieces

300 ml (about $^{1}/_{2}$ pt) beef stock (page 164)

salt

3 tbsp chopped parsley

Oyster blade steak is perfect here. It is one of the most delicious cuts for a stew. Ask your butcher to trim the fat off, but don't worry about any sinews you may see—these gelatinous bits keep the meat tender and tasty.

Place the meat in a bowl with the onion, thyme, bay leaf, parsley, garlic, clove and carrots. Add the wine and brandy, and season with pepper. Cover with plastic wrap and refrigerate for 6 hours.

Preheat the oven to 160°C/320°F. Remove the meat pieces, drain and pat dry with kitchen paper. Heat the oil and butter in a large frying pan and seal the meat on both sides. Transfer to an ovenproof casserole. Add the bacon to the frying pan, sauté for 3 minutes and then transfer to the casserole dish. Add the marinade to the frying pan, bring to the boil and then add this to the casserole with the stock. Season with a little salt and bring to a simmer. Cover the casserole and cook in the preheated oven for about 2 hours or until the meat is tender.

Remove from oven and skim the fat from the surface using a slotted spoon. Reduce oven temperature to 100°C/210°F. Transfer the meat, carrots and bacon to a deep serving dish, cover with foil and place in the oven to keep warm while you make the sauce.

Strain the cooking liquid into a wide-based saucepan, discarding the solids. Boil until it reduces and lightly coats the back of a wooden spoon. Season to taste and pour the sauce over the meat and vegetables. Sprinkle with parsley, and serve with a purée either of potato or celeriac and potato.

braised leg of lamb

with celery

SERVES 6

2 tbsp olive oil

a 1.5 kg (about 3 lb) leg of lamb, trimmed of
as much fat as possible

1 tbsp fresh rosemary

1 medium-sized brown onion, cut into
12 pieces

1 medium carrot, cut into 1 cm ($^1/_2$ in) dice

3 cloves garlic, crushed

salt and freshly ground black pepper

8–10 sticks of celery

$^1/_2$ cup white wine

One of those slow-cooked dishes perfect for a cold winter's evening. Accompany it with mashed potato, a good bottle of red wine and some fresh bread to soak up the sauce.

Preheat oven to 150°C/300°F. Heat the oil in a large, ovenproof casserole and brown the leg of lamb on all sides for a few minutes. Add the rosemary, onion, carrot and garlic, and season with salt and pepper. Cover with foil, then with a lid, and cook in the preheated oven for 2 hours. Baste twice during that time and turn the meat over.

Meanwhile, cut the celery into 5 cm (2 in) pieces and wash well (peel the tougher stalks). After the 2 hours has elapsed, add the celery to the dish with the wine. Season with a little extra salt and pepper, cover and cook for a further hour or so until the meat comes easily away from the bone.

rigatoni

with ratatouille

S E R V E S 4

1 red capsicum

3 tbsp olive oil

1 small brown onion, cut into 1 cm
(½ in) cubes

1 eggplant, cut into 1 cm (½ in) cubes

1 zucchini, cut into 1 cm (½ in) cubes

4 tomatoes, cut into 1 cm (½ in) cubes

2 sprigs of thyme, chopped

salt and freshly ground black pepper

400 g (about 14 oz) rigatoni

2 tbsp chopped parsley (optional)

4 tbsp finely grated parmesan

Ratatouille, the popular Provençale dish of zucchini, eggplant, capsicum and tomato, goes well with rigatoni. Cut into small cubes, the vegetables are just the right size to enter the tubes of pasta.

Halve the capsicum and remove the seeds. Cut the flesh into 1 cm (½ in) squares.

Heat 2 tablespoons of the oil over a medium heat in a wide non-stick pan and stir-fry the onion and capsicum for 2 minutes. Increase the heat, add the eggplant and stir-fry for a further 3–4 minutes. Add the zucchini, tomatoes and thyme, season with salt and pepper, and cook over a low heat for about 20 minutes.

Meanwhile, cook the pasta in a large amount of boiling salted water. Drain, then toss the pasta with the ratatouille, the remaining oil and the parsley. Serve sprinkled with the parmesan.

rabbit and red capsicum couscous

SERVES 6

2 rabbits, each weighing about 800 g (about 1$^{3}/_{4}$ lb)

2 tbsp olive oil

$^{1}/_{4}$ tsp cumin seeds

1 medium-sized onion, sliced

1 tbsp harissa (a North African chilli paste)

2 cloves garlic, crushed

1 tbsp tomato paste, diluted with a little water

4 medium-sized tomatoes, quartered

a 3 cm (1$^{1}/_{2}$ in) cinnamon stick

3 sprigs of parsley

3 red capsicums, quartered

3 medium-sized carrots, each cut into 6 pieces

salt and freshly ground black pepper

1 cup canned chickpeas, drained

3 cups couscous

2 tsp ground cumin

1 cup fresh coriander leaves

extra harissa for the table

A great dish to share on a cold day. Sweet, lean and tasty, rabbit meat appears regularly on our table at home. We love it and try it in many different ways. Here it is done with a North African touch.

Cut the rabbits into serving pieces. Heat the oil in a large pan. Stir in the cumin seeds and brown the rabbit pieces for a few minutes. Add onion, harissa, garlic, tomato paste, tomatoes, cinnamon, parsley, capsicums and carrots. Cover with cold water and season with salt and pepper. Bring to the boil and simmer for 1 hour.

Add chickpeas and simmer until the rabbit meat is cooked and is easily detached from the bone.

Follow the instructions on the couscous pack or, for the best result, first place the couscous in a fine strainer and run cold water over it for 2–3 minutes. Then use a damp cloth or muslin to line the perforated compartment of your steamer. Put in the wet couscous and bring the water in the steamer to the boil. Steam the couscous, uncovered, for about 15 minutes or until the grains are soft and hot.

Stir the ground cumin into the rabbit stew and season to taste with salt and pepper. Spoon the couscous onto a large platter or bowl and top with the rabbit pieces. Serve the vegetables and liquid in a separate bowl. Sprinkle the meat with coriander leaves and serve with extra harissa on the table.

jugged hare

with smoked bacon (civet de lièvre)

SERVES 6–8, DEPENDING ON
THE SIZE OF THE HARE

*A traditional casserole of hare
marinated in wine and herbs and then
cooked slowly until tender. The perfect
occasion to serve your most lovely,
full-bodied red wine. Don't buy a huge
hare, as it is likely to be tough.*

1 hare, weighing about 2 kg (4 lb)

1 medium-sized brown onion, sliced

1 medium-sized carrot, sliced

3 cloves garlic, crushed

1 bay leaf

2 cloves

10 whole black peppercorns, crushed

3 sprigs of thyme

2 tbsp cognac or brandy

600 ml (about 1 pt) good, full-bodied
red wine

1 tbsp vegetable oil

50 g (almost 2 oz) butter

a 400 g (about 14 oz) piece of smoked bacon,
cut into pieces 3 cm long and 1 cm thick

2 tbsp plain flour

3 sprigs of parsley

salt and freshly ground black pepper

3 tbsp chopped parsley

Cut off the hare's front and back legs. Cut the middle part into 4–5 pieces, cutting through the flesh first and then using a cleaver or large knife to cut through the bones. Place hare in a wide bowl, throw in the sliced onion and carrot, the garlic, bay leaf, cloves, peppercorns and thyme. Add the cognac and red wine, cover meat with foil and seal the bowl with plastic wrap. Refrigerate overnight or for at least 8 hours.

Drain the pieces of hare and dry them with kitchen paper. Strain the marinade liquid into a saucepan, reserving the vegetables.

Preheat oven to 160°C/320°F. In a wide, heavy casserole dish, heat the oil and half of the butter over a medium heat. Add the bacon, stir for 3 minutes, then transfer to a bowl. Add dried hare pieces to the pan and brown on all sides over a high heat. Transfer hare to a dish and add the remaining butter to pan. Add the reserved vegetables and herbs from the marinade and stir-fry for 3 minutes. Stir in the flour, cook for 2 minutes, then add the strained marinade liquid. Bring to a simmer, stirring well. Add meat, bacon and parsley sprigs, and shake the pan well. Season with extra salt, and add a little boiling water if needed to almost cover the meat. Cover with a lid and cook in the preheated oven for about 2 hours or until the meat can be easily detached from the bone.

Transfer meat and bacon to a deep serving dish and place in a warm oven (100°C/210°F). Strain the sauce into a saucepan, discarding the herbs and vegetables, and bring to the boil. Reduce the sauce by boiling over a medium heat until it is thick enough to coat the back of a wooden spoon. Season to taste. Pour sauce over meat and sprinkle with chopped parsley.

Steamed potatoes or fresh pasta are perfect accompaniments for this dish.

braised celery heart

with bacon

a bunch of celery, cut across 15 cm (6 in)
from the base

20 g (about ²/₃ oz) butter

¹/₂ tbsp olive oil

¹/₂ cup diced bacon

¹/₂ small brown onion, diced

1 medium-sized carrot, diced

3 sprigs of lemon thyme

1 cup veal or beef stock (page 164)

salt and freshly ground black pepper

2 tbsp chopped parsley

Celery heart is the base of the bunch, where the stalks meet. Vegetarians can replace the bacon with mushrooms and the veal stock with vegetable stock.

Peel the outer celery stalks to remove any large strings, and trim or remove any damaged stalks. Cut the celery heart into quarters lengthwise.

Heat the butter and oil in a casserole and stir-fry the bacon, onion, carrot and lemon thyme for 3 minutes. Add the celery and cook over a medium heat for 5 minutes. Add the stock, season with salt and pepper, and bring to a simmer. Cover with foil and a lid, and cook over a low heat for 10 minutes. Turn the celery over and cook for a further 10–15 minutes or until tender.

Sprinkle with parsley and serve with crusty bread.

curried lentils

with carrots

This is one of our family favourites. I like to use green lentils, because they stay firm after cooking.

SERVES 4

2 tbsp vegetable oil

1/2 brown onion, finely chopped

2 cloves garlic, finely chopped

1/2 tbsp finely grated ginger root

1/2 tsp cumin seeds

1/4 tsp black mustard seeds

2 cardamom pods

1/2 tbsp mild curry powder

300 g (about 11 oz) green lentils

1/2 cup Italian-style tomato sauce

2 medium-sized carrots, cut into 5 mm (about 1/4 in) slices

3 cups chicken stock (page 165)

salt and freshly ground black pepper

Heat the oil in a large saucepan over a medium heat and stir-fry the onion, garlic and ginger for 3 minutes. Add the cumin, mustard seeds and the cardamom, and stir for 1 minute. Stir in the curry powder, then add lentils, tomato sauce, carrots and chicken stock. Cover with water to 3 cm (11/2 in) above the vegetables and then simmer for 30–50 minutes, until tender. Add a little boiling water if necessary.

When the lentils are tender, season with salt and pepper. Serve with Indian bread or with rice cooked by the absorption method.

tagliatelle

with capsicum and olives

SERVES 4

1 red capsicum

1 yellow capsicum

400 g (about 14 oz) tagliatelle

2 tbsp olive oil

1/2 medium-sized brown onion, diced

1 clove garlic, finely chopped

2 tbsp finely chopped parsley

2 tbsp finely sliced fresh basil

20 black olives, pitted and cut into quarters

salt and freshly ground black pepper

4 tbsp grated parmesan

Preheat the griller. Place the whole capsicums on a baking sheet and position them about 5 cm (2 in) below the flame. Turn them when the skin has lightly browned. Once they are brown all over, remove from grill and wrap in foil for 15 minutes. (This traps moisture, which helps loosen the skins.) Peel and halve the capsicums, remove the seeds and cut the flesh into long strips. This part of the dish can be done in advance.

Cook the pasta in a large amount of boiling salted water. Meanwhile, heat half the oil in a frying pan. Add the onion and stir for 3 minutes. Add the capsicums, cook for 2 minutes, then toss in the garlic, parsley and basil. Add pasta with the remaining oil and the olives, and season with salt and pepper. Sprinkle with parmesan and serve.

alsatian sauerkraut

SERVES 6

1 kg (about 2 lb) sauerkraut ('sour cabbage')

20 g (about ²/₃ oz) butter

1 large brown onion, sliced

1 bay leaf

2 cloves

12 juniper berries

600 g (about 1¼ lb) kasseler, cut into 6 slices

6 slices jagdwurst or strassburg sausage, about 1 cm (½ in) thick

6 slices kaiserfleisch, about 1 cm (½ in) thick

½ bottle dry white wine, preferably Alsatian riesling

6 medium-sized potatoes

6 thin Viennese sausages or good quality frankfurts

3 tbsp chopped parsley

You'll often find this on the menu in brasseries in France. It's a wonderful winter dish to be served on a large platter in the centre of the table and enjoyed with an Alsatian riesling or a European beer.

Rinse the sauerkraut in cold water and squeeze out the excess moisture. This removes some of the sour taste.

Melt the butter in a wide saucepan and gently fry the onion for 3 minutes. Sprinkle half the sauerkraut on top and add the bay leaf, cloves and half the juniper berries. Arrange the slices of kasseler, jagdwurst and kaiserfleisch on top, then add the remaining sauerkraut and juniper berries. Pour the wine over, cover the pan tightly and simmer slowly for about 2 hours. (It can also be cooked in the oven at 150°C/300°F for 2 hours.)

Half an hour before serving, peel and boil the potatoes and cook the Viennese sausages in simmering water for about 10 minutes.

Serve the cabbage on a large platter. Arrange the cooked meats and sausages on top and surround with the potatoes. Sprinkle with parsley and serve with mustard or your favourite condiments.

SPICES

of life

Spices, the most magic of seasonings, have always summoned up wonderful images in my mind. When I taste a dish containing cardamom, I am instantly transported to the luscious, green tropical forests of southern India, where cardamon grows in abundance. A hint of cumin recalls the delicious seafood couscous I once ate in Djerba, an island off Tunisia in the Mediterranean.

A good range of spices is now widely available. Select fresh, firm-looking whole spices that are not blemished or discoloured. Ground spices should be in sealed packs, and have strong, natural colours. Always purchase small quantities of spices, just enough to last two or three months.

The advantage of becoming familiar with as many spices as possible is that it multiplies the possibilities of creating exciting dishes. With a new or unfamiliar spice, first chew or suck it on its own so you can memorise the taste. Don't be afraid: most spices are mild, sweet and fruity with warming overtones. Only a few, such as peppers and mustards, are hot and they are easy to recognise. Begin by cooking dishes containing only one spice. Try, for example, pan-fried lamb chops dusted with cumin, vegetables stir-fried with mustard seeds, or baked apples sprinkled with ground cinnamon. As your confidence grows be more adventurous: add a little chilli to the cumin-dusted chops, use fennel as well as mustard seeds with the stir-fried vegetables, and so on. It sure will spice up your life!

roast vegetables

4 small potatoes, peeled, or 2 large ones halved or quartered

4 pieces of pumpkin

2 medium-sized carrots, cut into 3 cm (1½ in) pieces

1 large sweet potato, peeled and cut into 4 pieces

2 tbsp olive oil

¼ tsp sweet paprika

a pinch of curry powder

salt and freshly ground black pepper

Melt-in-the-mouth and sweet. Roasting is a fabulous way to cook firm vegetables such as pumpkin, carrots, sweet potato and potatoes.

Preheat the oven to 200°C/400°F.

Place all the vegetables in a saucepan and cover with cold water. Bring to the boil and cook for 2 minutes. Drain well.

In a bowl combine the olive oil, paprika, curry powder, salt and pepper. Toss the vegetables in this seasoning.

Line a flat oven tray with baking paper and arrange the vegetables on it. Bake in the preheated oven for 30–40 minutes until tender turning the vegetables two or three times during that time.

chicken drumsticks with potatoes and rosemary

SERVES 4

800 g (about 1¾ lb) potatoes

4 tbsp olive oil

8 chicken drumsticks, skin on or off

sea salt and freshly ground black pepper

1 medium-sized brown onion, diced

1 tbsp finely chopped fresh rosemary

2 tbsp chopped parsley

Preheat oven to 200°C/400°F.

Peel potatoes and cut into 1.5 cm (¾ in) dice. Heat half the oil in a wide ovenproof pan and brown the chicken on all sides over a medium heat. Transfer chicken pieces to a plate and season with salt and pepper.

Add remaining oil to the pan and stir-fry the potato, onion and rosemary over a high heat for 5 minutes. (The potato and onion should brown slightly.) Season with salt and pepper, return chicken to the pan and stir briefly to distribute everything evenly. Cook, uncovered, in the preheated oven for 20 minutes or until the chicken and potato are tender. Stir once or twice during the cooking. Sprinkle with parsley just before serving.

chicken and fine herb risotto

4 cups chicken stock (page 165)

400 g (about 14 oz) boned skinless chicken thighs, sliced finely

salt and freshly ground black pepper

1 tbsp olive oil

½ onion, finely chopped

300 g (about 11 oz) arborio rice (Italian round-grain rice)

4 button mushrooms, finely sliced

2 tbsp dry white wine

2 tbsp chopped parsley

1 tbsp finely chopped fresh tarragon or basil

1 tbsp finely chopped fresh mint

2 tbsp freshly grated parmesan

20 g (about ⅔ oz) butter

Arborio rice, traditionally used for risotto, absorbs the flavour of other ingredients better than any other rice. Chicken stock is my first choice for making a risotto and when the dish is seasoned with fine herbs, as here, it is sublime.

Bring the stock to a simmer in a large saucepan. Add the chicken and cook for 4 minutes. Transfer chicken to a bowl and season with salt and pepper. Keep the stock simmering on the stove.

Heat the oil in a medium-sized saucepan and gently fry the onion for 3 minutes. Add the rice and mushrooms, and stir well for about a minute. Add the wine and boil for a minute to reduce. Add about a cup of chicken stock and bring to a simmer, stirring gently. Simmer until almost all the stock has been absorbed, then add another half cupful. Continue adding stock in this way, stirring occasionally to prevent the rice from sticking and to allow it to cook evenly. Check a few grains of rice from time to time: it takes about 20 minutes in total. You may not need to use all the stock; if, on the other hand, you don't have enough, add a little boiling water.

Add the chicken when the rice is cooked but still a little firm in the centre. The risotto should be creamy, but not runny. Gently stir in the herbs, parmesan and butter, and season to taste. Turn off the heat, cover the pan and leave to rest for about 5 minutes before serving.

chicken cooked in pinot noir
(coq au vin)

Serves 6

2 tbsp butter

300 g (about 11 oz) kassler or bacon, cut into pieces about 3 × 1 cm and 1 cm thick (1½ × ½ × ½ in)

½ bottle pinot noir or other red wine

6 chicken thighs, skin on or off

6 chicken drumsticks

salt and freshly ground black pepper

1 small brown onion, diced

2 tbsp plain flour

2 tbsp brandy

1 tbsp tomato paste

2 cloves garlic, crushed

1 cup strong chicken stock (page 165)

a bouquet garni of thyme, parsley and a bay leaf

½ cup Italian-style tomato sauce

2 tbsp chopped parsley

A tender and tasty free-range chicken slow-cooked in a good pinot noir is perfect for a weekend meal at the snow—for dinner anywhere on a cold winter's day, in fact.

The classic coq au vin can be varied in many ways. I prefer a red wine with strong fruit flavour and sometimes use all drumsticks or thighs. If you use fillets, cook the dish for ten minutes less or the meat will be dry.

Preheat the oven to 160°C/320°F.

Heat half the butter in a wide ovenproof dish and fry the bacon for 2–3 minutes. Transfer the bacon to a bowl and drain off the fat from the pan.

Bring the wine to the boil in a small saucepan. Season chicken pieces with salt and pepper. Add remaining butter to the pan in which you cooked the bacon, and brown the chicken pieces. Add onion, stir gently for 3 minutes, then sprinkle flour over chicken and cook for a further 2 minutes. Add the brandy, tomato paste and garlic, and gently stir in the hot wine and the stock. Add bouquet garni and tomato sauce, and bring to a simmer. Cover the dish and bake in the preheated oven for 30 minutes.

When the chicken is cooked, remove it from the liquid and transfer to a serving dish. Cover, and put in a warm oven (100°C/210°F).

Strain the cooking liquid into a saucepan, discarding the herbs and onion, and boil until you have a sauce thick enough to coat the back of a wooden spoon. Add the bacon pieces to reheat for 2 minutes, then spoon the sauce over chicken, sprinkle with chopped parsley and serve.

My favourite vegetables with a coq au vin are steamed peas and carrots and sautéed mushrooms.

roast free-range chicken

with tarragon

Simple pleasures are often the best and a roast free-range chicken definitely belongs in this category. Tarragon is the perfect herb to use, but if it is unavailable you can substitute rosemary or thyme.

SERVES 4

1 tsp finely chopped rosemary

1 tbsp olive oil

sea salt and freshly ground black pepper

a free-range chicken weighing about 1.5 kg (3 lb)

a handful of tarragon (stalks included)

1 medium-sized onion, diced

1 medium-sized carrot, diced

⅓ cup dry white wine

1 cup chicken stock (page 165)

2 tsp cornflour mixed with 1 tbsp water

Preheat the oven to 200°C/400°F.

Mix the rosemary with the olive oil and season with salt and pepper.

Season the cavity of the chicken with salt and pepper and place half the tarragon inside. Truss the legs of the chicken with kitchen string and rub the legs and breast with the olive oil and rosemary mixture.

Brown chicken on both sides (the leg side) for a few minutes in a roasting pan on top of the stove. Place the onion and carrot around the chicken in the pan and roast in the preheated oven for 20 minutes on one side. Turn the chicken onto the other leg, baste, then lower the heat to 160°C/350°F and roast for a further 20 minutes. Place chicken on its back, baste again and roast for a further 10 minutes. Transfer chicken to a serving dish, cover with foil and leave to rest while you make the sauce.

Drain excess fat from roasting pan, retaining the onion and carrot. Add the wine to the pan and bring to the boil for 1 minute, stirring well. Add the stock and remaining tarragon (keep a few leaves for garnish, if you wish). Return to the boil, cook for 1 minute, then whisk in the cornflour mixture and boil for a further 2 minutes. Season with salt and pepper, strain sauce into a small pan and keep hot over a low heat.

Cut the chicken into portions and serve with the sauce.

Roast butternut pumpkin and a green salad dressed with garlic, vinegar and olive oil are perfect accompaniments for this dish.

osso bucco

with lemon grass and saffron

It is exciting for a cook to prepare a dish using the ingredients and savoir-faire of more than one cuisine. Here you'll find the texture of a classic European meat dish coupled with a distinctive Asian flavour.

SERVES 4

a 10 cm (4 in) piece of lemon grass (root part)

2 cloves garlic

1 small brown onion, cut into pieces

1 small carrot, cut into pieces

3 medium-sized tomatoes, seeds removed and flesh cut into pieces

1.3 kg (about 2$\frac{1}{2}$ lb) shin of veal, cut into 3 cm (1$\frac{1}{2}$ in) slices

a little plain flour

salt and freshly ground black pepper

2 tbsp olive oil

$\frac{1}{4}$ tsp fennel seeds

$\frac{1}{3}$ cup dry white wine

2 pinches of saffron threads

2 tbsp finely chopped parsley or coriander

Preheat the oven to 190°C/350°F.

Cut the lemon grass in half lengthways and slice into small pieces. Place in a blender with the garlic, onion and carrot, and blend until very finely chopped. Separately blend the tomatoes to a fine purée.

Lightly coat the veal pieces with flour and season with salt and pepper. Heat the oil in a wide-based ovenproof casserole and brown the veal over a medium heat. Remove the meat from the dish and add the onion and carrot mixture and the fennel seeds. Stir well and cook for 3 minutes. Add wine and bring to the boil, then add the tomato purée and the saffron. Return the veal to the dish and add a little water to almost cover the meat. Bring to simmer, cover and cook in the preheated oven for about 1 hour or until the meat is easily detached from the bone. Season to taste with extra salt and pepper. Reduce oven temperature to 100°C/210°F. Transfer meat to a serving dish, cover and place in the oven to keep warm.

Boil the cooking juices for a few minutes until reduced to a sauce consistency. Spoon this over the meat and sprinkle with the parsley or coriander. Serve with spinach, baby carrots and rice.

sweet *endings*

Like many French children, I loved helping my grandmother make cakes and desserts. I was fascinated with the whole process and, of course, couldn't wait to share the cake later on. My grandmother was a talented cake-maker and I remember being amazed at her range of differently shaped cake and tart moulds, and her huge rolling-pin and pastry cutters. She always encouraged us to help, inviting us to weigh the ingredients in her old-fashioned scales, grease the moulds, stir a cream or mix a dough. Licking the wooden spoons was, naturally, the best part. My older brother later became a boulanger–pâtissier and I became a chef with a penchant for making cakes and desserts—all thanks to Grand'mère.

Since most cakes and desserts can be prepared in advance, it is easy to be relaxed about and enjoy baking. As quantities need to be exact for best results, it is worthwhile investing in scales and measuring cups and spoons. A good electric mixer is always a pleasure to use, and good-quality cake tins and moulds simplify the task even further.

As with all cooking, always use the freshest of ingredients for cake-making. Fresh free-range eggs taste infinitely better than battery eggs, and good-quality butter and chocolate make a big difference to the fragrance and flavour of your cake. When using self-raising flour or yeast, always check the use-by date. On hot days, cool your flour and sugar in the fridge for fifteen minutes before mixing them with other ingredients.

Although it can be time-consuming, making pastries, soufflés, custards and ice-creams is extremely satisfying. If you feel daunted by the idea, practise on your family when you are not under pressure. Make sure you allow enough time for the preparations, and always measure your ingredients with precision.

chocolate dacquoise

A dacquoise consists of layers of meringue encasing a rich, chocolatey filling. The meringue can be prepared a day or two in advance, and the cake assembled on the day you need it. Once assembled it keeps well for 36 hours.

SERVES 8–10

MERINGUE

80 g (about 3 oz) hazelnut meal

240 g (about 8 oz) caster sugar

1½ tbsp cornflour

6 egg whites (size 55 eggs)

a pinch of cream of tartar

2 drops red wine vinegar

3 drops vanilla essence

½ cup roasted hazelnuts, crushed into 2 or 3 pieces

FILLING AND FINISHING

1 cup thickened cream

300 g (about 11 oz) dark cooking chocolate, cut into small pieces

icing sugar for dusting the cake

You will need a piping bag fitted with a 1 cm (½ in) plain nozzle.

Line one or two large oven trays with baking paper, then draw three circles, 20 cm (8 in) in diameter, onto the paper. Preheat the oven to 180°C/350°F.

Lightly toast the hazelnut meal in a dry pan for a few minutes over a medium heat. Transfer to a bowl to cool, then mix into it the cornflour and about ¼ cup of the caster sugar.

Using an electric mixer, beat the egg whites and cream of tartar on a medium-high speed until almost stiff. At low speed, gradually add the remaining caster sugar and then the vinegar and vanilla essence, and continue to beat until stiff peaks form.

Fold the hazelnut mixture into the beaten egg whites. Fill a piping bag with this mixture and pipe three flat rounds inside the drawn circles on the baking paper: start from the outside and move inwards to fill the shapes. Sprinkle half the crushed hazelnuts onto one of the rounds, then bake the disks in the preheated oven for about 30 minutes or until the meringue is firm and dry. (If preparing the meringue in advance, allow to cool and then store in an airtight container.)

Bring the cream to the boil in a saucepan. Remove from the heat and stir in the chocolate until it has melted and the mixture is smooth. Allow this filling (the ganache) to cool, but don't let it set.

Stir the remaining hazelnuts into the ganache and spread one of the plain meringue disks (without hazelnuts on top) with almost half this mixture. Place the second plain meringue disk on top and spread with almost all the remaining ganache (reserve 4–5 tablespoons). Top with the last disk, the hazelnuts facing upwards. Heat the remaining ganache briefly to soften it, then use a spatula to spread it around the sides of the cake. Sprinkle the top with icing sugar before serving.

quatre-quarts butter cake

My grandmother used to make this cake as a weekend treat. Quatre-quarts means 'four quarters': the cake consists of a quarter sugar, a quarter eggs, a quarter butter and a quarter flour. It is one of the simplest cakes to make.

SERVES 8–12

butter and flour for the cake tin

180 g (about 6 oz) sugar

3 eggs, about 60 g each

2 tsp finely grated lemon zest

180 g (about 6 oz) butter, just melted

180 g (about 6 oz) plain flour

You need a 23 cm (9 in) round cake tin or a 20 cm (8 in) square tin, greased with butter and dusted with flour.

Preheat the oven to 180°C/350°F. Beat the sugar, eggs and zest until creamy. Mix in the melted butter, then sift the flour over the top and fold in until just mixed. (Don't overwork it.) Pour the mixture into tin and bake in the preheated oven for about 30 minutes: a skewer inserted should come out clean.

Allow the cake to cool in the tin for about 5 minutes before turning it out onto a rack. It is even more delicious with a strawberry or passionfruit icing.

a delicious sponge

The texture of a sponge makes it perhaps the most popular of all cakes, and the aroma wafting from the kitchen as it bakes is out of this world.

SERVES 8–10

butter and flour for the cake tin

6 free-range eggs (size 60)

180 g (about 6 oz) caster sugar

2 tsp finely grated lemon zest

100 g (about 3½ oz) plain flour, sifted

80 g (about 3 oz) butter, just melted

Preheat the oven to 180°C/350°F. Grease and flour a 25 cm (10 in) round cake tin.

Put the eggs, sugar and lemon zest in a large bowl and, using an electric beater, beat until the mixture forms a thick ribbon (this takes about 8 minutes).

Add the sifted flour all at once and use a rubber spatula to fold it in gently but quickly. (Do not overmix.) Gently incorporate the melted butter, again not overmixing. Pour the mixture into the prepared tin, tap the tin gently to eliminate air bubbles, and smooth the top with a spatula. Bake in the preheated oven for 40 minutes. Test the sponge by pressing lightly in the centre: if it springs back, it is done. Or test it with a skewer, which should come out clean.

Leave the cake to cool in the tin for 10 minutes before turning it out onto a rack.

banana and pineapple cake

MAKES 12 SLICES

1¹⁄₂ cups self-raising flour, sifted

¹⁄₂ tsp salt

¹⁄₂ cup almond meal

125 g (about ¹⁄₄ lb) butter and a little extra for greasing the tin

³⁄₄ cup caster sugar

2 eggs

1 tbsp milk

¹⁄₂ tsp bicarbonate of soda

2 bananas, mashed

¹⁄₂ cup puréed pineapple flesh

ICING

20 g (almost 1 oz) butter

50 g (almost 2 oz) cream cheese

1 tbsp lemon or pineapple juice

150 g (about 5 oz) icing sugar

Children love this cake, which is more a morning or afternoon treat than a dessert. Everyone seems to enjoy the cream-cheese icing.

You need a buttered loaf tin (or other tin of your choice), 20 cm × 12 cm (8 in × 5 in). Line the base with greased baking paper.

Preheat the oven to 160°C/320°F.

Combine the flour, salt and almond meal.

Beat the butter and sugar until well combined. Beat in the eggs one at a time, then beat in the milk which you have mixed with the bicarbonate of soda. Fold in the mashed banana and puréed pineapple.

Add flour mixture without overmixing. Spoon into the prepared tin and tap it gently to eliminate air bubbles. Flatten the top, then bake in the preheated oven for about 1 hour: a skewer inserted should come out clean.

Remove from the oven and leave to cool for 10 minutes before carefully unmoulding the cake onto a wire rack.

To make the icing, beat the butter with the cream cheese, lemon juice and icing sugar. Ice the cake when it is cold.

mango and passionfruit tart

The best mangoes I have ever tasted are Australian and this dish should be made when mangoes are at their peak, usually around Christmas. If you wish, make small tartlets instead of a large tart, especially for a dinner party.

SERVES 8

1 quantity of sweet pastry (page 174)

2 large mangoes

6 passionfruits

$^3/_4$ cup pure cream

2 tbsp full-cream milk

20 g (about $^2/_3$ oz) caster sugar

You need a tart mould about 25 cm (10 in) in diameter and 3 cm ($1^1/_2$ in) high.

Preheat the oven to 200°C/400°F.

Press down on the pastry a little with the palm of your hand to soften it before rolling. Roll it out on a well-floured surface to a thickness of 3–5 mm ($^1/_8$–$^1/_4$ in). Carefully wrap the pastry around the rolling pin to lift it onto the tart mould. Line the mould, gently patting the base and sides and trimming the edges with your fingertips. (There'll be some unused pastry, so if the flan pastry tears or breaks, patch it up as you would do with playdough.) Prick plenty of holes in the base and sides of the pastry, using a fork. Bake in the preheated oven for about 10 minutes or until the sides and base are golden-brown.

Remove from the oven and leave to cool before unmoulding.

Peel the mangoes. Using a sharp knife, cut them into 2 mm (about $1^1/_2$ in) slices, then into 1 cm ($^1/_2$ in) strips. Place in a bowl, then halve the passionfruits and scoop the flesh into the same bowl. Mix well and refrigerate.

Whip the cream and milk together. Mix in the sugar, and refrigerate. Just before serving, spread the whipped cream over the cold pastry base and top with the mango and passionfruit. Show it to your guests before slicing it: the fruits are so soft and slippery that the slices won't be really neat. But then who cares—it is delicious!

flourless chocolate, orange

and hazelnut cake

60 g (about 2 oz) sultanas

1 tbsp finely grated orange zest

2 tbsp Grand Marnier

1 tbsp melted butter to grease the tin

a little potato flour to dust the tin

180 g (about 6 oz) roasted hazelnuts

$\frac{1}{3}$ cup cream

160 g (about 5$\frac{1}{2}$ oz) dark cooking chocolate, broken into small pieces

4 eggs, separated

100 g (about 3$\frac{1}{2}$ oz) caster sugar

a pinch of cream of tartar

icing sugar to dust the cake

A chocoholic's delight, this flourless cake holds wonderful surprises—crunchy roasted hazelnuts and plump sultanas soaked in Grand Marnier. Perfect for morning or afternoon tea, or for dessert.

Preheat the oven to 180°C/350°F. Combine the sultanas, orange zest and Grand Marnier in a bowl.

Grease a 23 cm (9 in) spring-form cake tin with melted butter, line the base with greased baking paper and dust the tin with potato flour.

Blend 100 g (about 3$\frac{1}{2}$ oz) of hazelnuts very finely, almost to a flour. Use the base of a saucepan to crush the remaining nuts each into 3 or 4 pieces and spread these over the base of cake tin.

Put the cream in a small saucepan and bring to the boil. Remove from heat and stir in the chocolate until it melts. Using an electric mixer, beat the egg yolks and sugar until fluffy and white (this takes about 4 minutes). Add the chocolate mixture, ground hazelnuts, sultana mixture, and combine gently.

Beat the egg whites with the cream of tartar until the mixture forms stiff peaks. Fold into the chocolate mixture, then pour into the cake tin. Gently flatten the top and bake in the preheated oven for 50 minutes or until cooked: a skewer inserted should come out clean.

Allow the cake to cool for about 20 minutes before carefully unmoulding it onto a rack. Dust generously with icing sugar.

Serve with vanilla ice-cream, rich cream, a crème anglaise or a raspberry sauce.

baked lemon cheesecake

SERVES 12

120 g (about 4 oz) plain sweet biscuits,
crushed to the texture of sugar

80 g (about 3 oz) melted butter

2 tbsp almonds, very finely chopped

1¾ cups milk

60 g (about 2 oz) unsalted butter

60 g (about 2 oz) cornflour

2 egg yolks

350 g (about 12½ oz) cream cheese

juice of 2 lemons

5 egg whites

a pinch of cream of tartar

150 g (about 5 oz) caster sugar

icing sugar for dusting

I owe my love of cheesecakes to my adopted country, Australia, for I never made them in France. This is my favourite version and the lightest in my repertoire.

Preheat the oven to 150°C/300°F.

Butter a 24 cm (about 9 in) springform cake tin.

Using a wooden spoon, combine the biscuit crumbs, melted butter and chopped almonds. Using the back of the spoon, press this mixture onto the base and two-thirds up the sides of the prepared tin. Refrigerate while you prepare the filling.

Bring 1⅓ cups of the milk to the boil with the butter. Meanwhile, combine the cornflour, egg yolks and remaining milk in a bowl. Add this to the hot milk, mix well and cook over a low heat for about 5 minutes. Remove from the heat, stir in the cream cheese and then the lemon juice, and mix until very smooth.

Beat the egg whites with the cream of tartar until the mixture forms stiff peaks. Add sugar little by little and continue beating until the egg whites are firm. Fold gently into the cream-cheese mixture and pour into the mould, gently flattening the top. Bake in preheated oven for 1 hour 20 minutes.

Allow to cool completely before unmoulding. Dust with a little icing sugar before serving.

blueberry coeur à la crème

S ERVES 6

500 g (about 1 lb) blueberries, raspberries
or blackberries

200 g (about 7 oz) sugar

2 tbsp water

1 cup pure cream

2 tbsp milk

300 g (about 11 oz) fromage blanc (quark or
smooth creamed cottage cheese)

juice of 1 lemon

A creamy, fruity dessert of the palest mauve colour and shaped like a heart. This has to be food for lovers. You need a 20 cm (8 in) porcelain coeurs à la crème mould and a piece of muslin about 60 cm (24 in) square.

Place the blueberries, sugar and water in a food processor and blend to a purée. Transfer the purée to a saucepan, bring to the boil and simmer for 10 minutes. Strain into a bowl and allow to cool.

When the blueberry sauce is cold, whip the cream and milk together until the mixture just starts to stiffen. Blend the fromage blanc with one-third of the blueberry sauce and the lemon juice, until smooth. Gently but thoroughly combine this mixture with the whipped cream.

Line the mould with a damp muslin cloth and rest the mould in a dish. Fill with the mixture and close the muslin over the top. Refrigerate for 3 hours, during which time the excess water will drain out. Gently unmould dessert onto a dish and serve with the blueberry sauce.

almond and blueberry galette

A rich, fruity cake featuring the intense flavour of blueberries trapped inside a buttery almond pastry. Best enjoyed for morning or afternoon tea or with a glass of champagne or sauternes.

SERVES 8

160 g (about 5½ oz) plain flour, sifted

80 g (about 3 oz) almond meal

200 g (about 7 oz) butter, cut into small cubes

2 tsp finely grated lemon zest

200 g (about 7 oz) caster sugar

4 egg yolks

50 g (almost 2 oz) flaked almonds

200 g (about 7 oz) blueberries, washed

Place the flour and almond meal in a bowl, making a well in the centre. Put the butter, lemon zest, sugar and 3½ egg yolks (keep half a yolk for the glaze) in the well. Using your fingertips, work the wet ingredients together until just combined, then gradually incorporate the flour and almond meal. Shape the dough into a ball, using a table knife to scrape the mixture from your hands, and refrigerate for about 30 minutes.

Preheat the oven to 200°C/400°F. Butter a 25 cm (10 in) flan tin and sprinkle the inside with the flaked almonds.

Cut the dough in half. Lightly flour the dough, your hands and the rolling pin then roll each half out into a circle to fit the tin. Place one round of dough in the flan tin and top with the blueberries, leaving a 1 cm margin around the edge. Place the other round of dough on top and brush with the remaining half egg yolk, lightly beaten with 1 teaspoon of water. Use a fork to draw a criss-cross pattern on top. Bake in the preheated oven for 20 minutes, then lower the temperature to 180°C/350°F and bake for a further 35 minutes. Leave to cool before unmoulding with care. Serve with cream, ice-cream or a fruit sauce.

dutch cocoa sauce

MAKES ABOUT 1½ CUPS (8–10 SERVES)

¾ cup water

60 g (about 2 oz) caster sugar

120 g (about 4 oz) Dutch cocoa

¾ cup cream

A delightful sauce for those who love the taste of bitter chocolate. You can adapt it to your taste by using more sugar or cream or, for a special touch, adding toasted chopped nuts such as hazelnuts or almonds just before serving. You can also flavour it with Grand Marnier, Cointreau or Kirsch, or with whisky or cognac.

Bring the water, sugar and cocoa to the boil in a saucepan, stirring well to dissolve everything thoroughly. Add the cream and boil for 20 seconds.

Use immediately or allow to cool, cover and refrigerate.

apple and cinnamon fritters

This is a family dessert par excellence. If you are making the fritters for adults, try marinating the apple slices (for 20 minutes before cooking) in 50 g (almost 2 oz) caster sugar, 2 tablespoons calvados or other liqueur and the juice of half a lemon.

SERVES 4

100 g (about 3½ oz) plain flour, sifted

1 egg

1 tbsp olive oil

¼ tsp salt

2 tsp caster sugar

⅓ cup beer

about 3 cups vegetable oil

3 medium-sized apples

½ tsp ground cinnamon

icing sugar or caster sugar for dusting

Place the flour in a bowl and make a well in the centre. Pour the egg, oil, salt and sugar into the well and combine these four ingredients first. Add the flour and beer alternately, mixing until they are incorporated and the batter is smooth and thin. (You may have some beer left over.) Cover the bowl and leave to stand for about 2 hours.

Heat the vegetable oil to 180°C/350°F. If you don't have an oil thermometer, test the oil by placing a few drops of batter in the pan: they should float to the surface and turn brown almost straight away.

Peel and core the apples and cut into 8 mm (nearly ⅓ in) slices, each with a hole in the centre. Dust the slices with cinnamon. Dip several apple slices into the batter to coat them lightly, then use a fork to lift them into the oil. Fry for about 3 minutes, turning each slice over half-way through. Drain and place on kitchen paper.

When all the fritters are cooked, dust with icing sugar or caster sugar and serve hot. They are lovely with lemon or with jam and cream.

sablés

with cardamom-poached cherries

A fragrant dessert of alternating layers of biscuit, cherries and cream. The delicate little biscuits are made with shortbread pastry. They and the poached cherries can be prepared in advance.

S ERVES 4

a little plain flour

200 g (about 7 oz) sweet pastry (page 174)

$^3/_4$ cup water

3 tbsp sugar

6 cardamom pods

$^1/_4$ vanilla pod

400 g (about 14 oz) cherries, washed and pitted

$^1/_3$ cup whipping cream

icing sugar for dusting

Preheat the oven to 180°C/350°F.

Dust the work bench with the flour and roll out the pastry to a thickness of 3 mm ($^1/_8$ in). Using a fork, prick the pastry every 2–3 cm (1–1$^1/_2$ in). With a pastry cutter, cut 12 pastry rounds about 8 cm (3 in) in diameter and place them carefuly on a baking sheet lined with baking paper.

Bake in the preheated oven for about 8 minutes until lightly browned. Remove from the oven and allow to cool.

Bring the water, sugar, cardamom and vanilla to the boil in a medium saucepan and simmer for 5 minutes. Add the cherries and poach gently, stirring occasionally, until they are soft. Transfer cherries to a bowl and continue to boil the liquid until it reduces by half. Pour over the cherries and allow to cool. When cold, cover and refrigerate.

Place one biscuit on each of four dessert plates. Top with a tablespoon of whipped cream and a few cherries. Add another biscuit, more cream and cherries, finishing with a biscuit. Dust with icing sugar and, if you wish, decorate with fresh cherries.

minted poached quinces

4 cups water

¼ vanilla pod

grated zest of 1 orange

grated zest of 1 lemon

300 g (about 11 oz) sugar

3 medium-sized quinces, peeled and quartered

2 tbsp non-alcoholic peppermint syrup

I spent much of my youth playing under a handsome quince tree that produced hundreds of kilos of fruit every year. We made huge quantities of quince jelly, much of which we gave away. Serve this with either cream or ice-cream, with a crème anglaise (page 176) or even a chocolate sauce (page 136). You'll find the peppermint syrup at good grocery stores and some wine shops.

Place the water in a pan with the vanilla pod, orange and lemon zest, and sugar. Bring to the boil and simmer for 10 minutes. Add the quinces and simmer for a further 20 minutes. Add the peppermint syrup and simmer for 2 minutes, then turn off the heat. Refrigerate when cold, leaving the fruits to infuse in the syrup for 24 hours.

Before serving, drain the fruit and serve with 2 tablespoons of syrup per person. If you serve another sauce, don't serve the syrup.

peppermint crème brûlée

Mint gives a fresh flavour to this popular dessert. It is rich, so a small serve is quite enough. I like to use a non-alcoholic peppermint syrup: the French brands are excellent.

SERVES 6

4 egg yolks

150 g (about 5 oz) caster sugar

1 cup pure cream

180 ml (about ⅓ pt) full-cream milk

1 tbsp non-alcoholic peppermint syrup

40 g (about 1½ oz) brown sugar

Preheat oven to 160°C/320°F.

You need 6 half-cup porcelain soufflé moulds.

In a bowl, combine the egg yolks with two-thirds of the caster sugar. Add the cream, milk and peppermint syrup, and mix well.

Place soufflé moulds in a deep oven tray and pour the mixture into the moulds, using a ladle or jug. Two-thirds fill the tray with hot water, then carefully place it in the preheated oven and cook for 40 minutes. Remove from the oven and allow to cool in the liquid. Refrigerate the custards once cold, if you are not serving them immediately.

Mix the remaining caster sugar with the brown sugar and sprinkle evenly on top of the custards. Place under a hot grill until the sugar has caramelised, then serve.

passionfruit mousse

SERVES 6

³/₄ cup passionfruit pulp (6–10 passionfruits)

a 10 g (about ¹/₃ oz) sachet of gelatine powder

150 g (about 5 oz) sugar

2 tbsp water

3 egg whites

a pinch of cream of tartar

³/₄ cup cream, whipped

icing sugar for dusting

A delicate mousse made with beaten egg whites and a sugar syrup (known as Italian meringue mixture). To cook the syrup at the right temperature, you need a sugar thermometer: if you don't have one, cook the sugar and water over a medium heat for about 8 minutes until the mixture is slightly yellow. When you dip a teaspoonful of the syrup into cold water, it should harden a bit.

Heat the passionfruit pulp without boiling it. Remove from the heat and whisk in the gelatine until it has completely dissolved.

Put the sugar and water in a small saucepan and bring to the boil. Place the sugar thermometer in the pan and cook over a medium heat for 7–10 minutes or until the temperature reaches 121°C/248°F. Remove from heat immediately.

Using an electric mixer, beat the egg whites and cream of tartar until they form stiff peaks. Continuing to beat at low speed, very slowly pour the syrup in a thin stream over the whites, taking care not to let it run into the beater whisk. Beat for about 8 minutes or until the mixture is almost completely cold. Fold in the passionfruit mixture and then the whipped cream. Spoon into individual moulds or glasses, and refrigerate for at least 3 hours. Serve dusted with icing sugar and, if you wish, accompanied by diced fresh fruits.

HAIGH

CHOCOLATE

Chocolate releases several mood-boosting chemicals, including one called phenylethylamine that is very like the one produced in our bloodstream when we are in love. No wonder we adore the stuff! Chocolate is the product of a long process that begins on the rich, hilly slopes of dense tropical forests 400–800 metres above sea level, where the delicate cocoa tree grows in the warm shade of larger plants. The cocoa pod, the fruit of the tree, resembles an elongated pawpaw and is ripe when its colour has changed from purplish-red to orange. Fruit is produced all year round.

Skilled workers harvest the pods using sharp knives attached to long poles. The pods are cut open and the beans are scooped out, covered with banana leaves and left to ferment. It is during this stage that the cocoa aroma is released. Next the beans are dried in the sun, then inspected, graded and packed into jute sacks for transporting to chocolate-makers around the world. As with wine, coffee and olive oil, chocolate producers offer different varieties and qualities for particular markets.

The chocolate-maker roasts the beans before removing the outer husks, to reveal small kernels known as nibs. The nibs are ground into a thick aromatic paste known as chocolate liquor or mass. This is combined with other ingredients, such as sugar, and the mix blended until smooth. Finally, the chocolate is moulded ready for eating or for cooking. What a long journey!

french pancakes

with raspberry jam

250 g (about 9 oz) plain flour, sifted

a pinch of salt

1 tsp sugar

2 eggs (size 61 g)

2 cups milk

½ tbsp vegetable oil

1 tbsp butter

250 g (about 9 oz) raspberry jam

a few lemon wedges

pure cream or ice-cream

The thin, melt-in-the-mouth pancakes that all French families enjoy occasionally as a quick treat. It was a tradition in my youth for all members of the family to personally cook their own pancakes.

Place the flour, salt and sugar in a mixing bowl. Make a well in the centre and add the eggs and a third of the milk. Whisk the eggs and milk together, then gradually incorporate the flour, slowly whisking in the remaining milk to form a smooth thin batter. Refrigerate for 15–20 minutes, then pour through a fine strainer into a jug.

Heat the oil and butter over a medium heat, in a non-stick frying pan or a crêpe pan. When the butter turns golden, whisk it into the crêpe batter. Return the pan to the heat and pour in enough batter to thinly cover the base, tilting the pan to help the batter to spread evenly. When the upper half of the crêpe starts to dry and the lower half is lightly browned, turn the crêpe quickly using a spatula. After lightly browning the second side, transfer the crêpe to a plate. Make the rest of the crêpes in the same way. If they begin to stick, wipe the pan and melt in a little extra butter.

Spread some jam on one side of each crêpe. Fold it in half, then in half again to form a wedge. Dust with icing sugar or serve with lemon, cream or ice-cream.

baked peaches

with a strawberry sauce

SERVES 4

80 g (about 3 oz) caster sugar

40 g (about 1 1/2 oz) brown sugar

250 g (about 9 oz) ripe strawberries

4 ripe peaches

30 g (about 1 oz) butter

2 1/2 tbsp Kirsch

A treat for summer, when peaches are at their best. If you wish, replace the peaches with apricots, the strawberries with raspberries and the Kirsch with Drambuie.

Preheat the oven to 200°C/400°F.

Grease a porcelain oven dish with butter, then sprinkle it with a third each of the caster sugar and brown sugar.

Wash and hull the strawberries and cut into small cubes. Add to the dish. Wash and halve the peaches, remove the stones and then place skin-side down, on top of the strawberries. Sprinkle with remaining sugar and dot with small knobs of butter. Bake in the preheated oven for 20 minutes or until the peaches are cooked.

Bring the Kirsch to the boil in a small pan. Pour over the hot peaches and light with a match. For this to work, the Kirsch and the peaches must be very hot.

caramelised quince tart with star anise

An exotic version of that scrumptious classic, tarte tatin, for which apple is cooked in a caramel, puff pastry is baked over the top and the whole thing is turned upside-down before serving.

SERVES 6–8

5 quinces

50 g (almost 2 oz) butter

150 g (about 5 oz) caster sugar

2 star anise, broken into small pieces

300 g (about 11 oz) puff pastry (page 175)

Preheat oven to 200°C/400°F.

Peel, quarter and core the quinces. Place the butter, sugar and star anise in an ovenproof skillet over a medium heat. Carefully arrange the quince quarters in a single layer in the pan. Cook for about 15 minutes until the quinces are soft and lightly caramelised, lowering the heat if they caramelise too quickly.

Roll out the puff pastry about 3–5 mm (1/8–1/4 in) thick into a circle and large enough to cover the fruit in the skillet. Prick the pastry with a fork and then lay it delicately over the quinces. Trim the pastry edges and bake in the preheated oven until the pastry is cooked (15–20 minutes).

Remove the tart from the oven and let it stand for about 15 minutes. Pass the blade of a thin knife around the inside edge of the pan, place a serving platter upside-down on top and gently turn both over to unmould the tart. Serve hot or cold.

tart of fresh apricots

SERVES 8–12

1 quantity of sweet pastry (page 174)

a little plain flour

1 quantity of crème pâtissière (page 176)

1/3 cup cream, whipped

1 kg (about 2 lb) fresh apricots, washed and halved

3 tbsp caster sugar

You need a 28 cm (12 in) buttered spring-form tin.

Preheat the oven to 220°C/450°F. Remove the pastry from the fridge and press it down with your hand to make it easier to roll out. Dust the bench with a little flour and roll out the pastry to a circle to fit your tin and about 4 mm (almost 1/4 in) thick. Gently wrap the pastry around the rolling pin and lay it over the tin. Lightly press the base and sides into the tin and trim the edges with your fingertips. This pastry is fragile so if it breaks, just patch it up with extra bits of pastry. Prick holes in the base, using a fork.

Mix the cold crème pâtissière with the whipped cream. Spoon a 1 cm (1/2 in) layer of this mixture over the pastry. Cover with the apricot halves, skin-side down, starting from the outside and working inwards, and packing the apricots tightly. Dust with caster sugar and bake in the preheated oven for 15 minutes. Then lower the temperature to 150°C/300°F and bake for a further 20–30 minutes or until the pastry sides and base are lightly browned. Allow to cool for about 20 minutes before serving lukewarm or cold.

chocolate crème caramel

The classic crème caramel can be infused with many different flavourings, such as coffee, vanilla, lemon, orange and peppermint. Our children have a weakness for chocolate, but if you wish to keep it plain, just omit the cocoa. You need eight small porcelain soufflé moulds each holding about 150 ml, or twelve 100 ml moulds.

MAKES 8–12

2½ tbsp water

½ tsp red wine vinegar

400 g (about 14 oz) caster sugar

½ vanilla bean, split lengthwise

4 cups full-cream milk

2 tbsp Dutch cocoa

6 eggs

Bring the water, vinegar and half of the sugar to the boil in a small saucepan and cook until it turns golden. I prefer not to stir during the cooking, but keep an eye on things as caramel can burn very quickly once it starts to brown. Carefully pour some caramel into each mould to coat the base, tilting the mould to spread the caramel more easily.

Preheat oven to 160°C/320°F. Bring vanilla bean and milk to the boil in a saucepan, then whisk in the cocoa until melted. Thoroughly combine the eggs and remaining caster sugar in a bowl (don't beat it, as this creates too many bubbles). Gently whisk the hot milk into the egg mixture, combining well. Remove the vanilla bean.

Put the caramel-coated moulds in a deep oven tray. Using a jug or ladle, pour the mixture into the moulds. Two-thirds fill the roasting tray with hot water, then place it carefully in the preheated oven. Cook the larger moulds for 30–40 minutes and the smaller ones for 25–30 minutes. When the custards are set, they are cooked: test by shaking them lightly. Remove from the oven and allow to cool in the water before refrigerating.

Crème caramel is best eaten 24 hours after being made. It can be served in the mould or unmoulded (by running a blade around the inside edge of the mould) onto plates.

COFFEE

Coffee is much more than a stimulating drink. It is also one of the most beautiful flavours used in dessert-making. At any French pâtisserie the coffee éclairs are probably the most popular pastry, and at Italian gelaterias the coffee ice-cream is an enduring favourite.

Depending on the recipe, you need coffee flavouring in different forms. The Italian favourite, tiramisu, is made using fresh coffee. If you are preparing a mousse or ice-cream, or flavouring a crème pâtissière or crème anglaise, you can use either diluted instant coffee or a liquid coffee essence or extract, which is what the professionals use.

Coffee is a tropical plant and two species—coffea arabica and coffea robusta—provide most of the world's production. Arabica is an elongated, flat oval bean and has a lovely mild, aromatic flavour. The robusta plant has a smaller, more irregular bean with a more bitter taste and contains over twice as much caffeine as arabica.

Once coffee beans have been harvested, the pulp around them is carefully removed and the beans are hulled, graded and bagged ready for roasting. The roasting process is important, for it enhances the particular flavour characteristics of the coffee. If roasted too lightly, the coffee will be weak in flavour; if the beans are too dark, it will be bitter.

The roasted beans are stored in sealed bags or jars. Once opened, coffee deteriorates rapidly and it should therefore be purchased in small quantities. A good coffee retailer will sell you a blend to satisfy your needs and taste. They way the beans are ground depends on the method you use to make your coffee: the finest texture is suitable for espresso machines, while the coarser grinds are for plungers and percolators. Remember always to use a good-quality water with no unpleasant chemical flavours.

raspberry jelly

with granny smith sauce

SERVES 6

500 g (about 1 lb) raspberries

250 g (about 9 oz) caster sugar

1 vanilla bean, split lengthwise

1 cup cold water

10 g (about $\frac{1}{3}$ oz) gelatine powder

3 Granny Smith apples

extra $\frac{1}{3}$ cup cold water

Reserve 18 whole raspberries for decoration. Place the remaining berries in a saucepan with 200 g (about 7 oz) of the sugar, half the vanilla bean and the water. Boil for 5 minutes, then remove the vanilla bean and scrape the tiny black seeds into the juice. Blend the raspberry mixture to a purée, then pass it through a fine strainer. Return it to the pan and simmer for 5 minutes. Remove from heat and whisk in the gelatine, stirring until it dissolves. Allow the mixture to cool and pour into a large jelly mould, individual moulds or six wine glasses. Refrigerate for 3–4 hours until set.

Peel, quarter and core the apples. Place in a saucepan with the remaining sugar, the extra water and the other half of the vanilla bean. Bring to the boil and simmer until the apples are soft. Remove the vanilla bean and blend the apples to a fine purée. Allow to cool.

To serve, unmould the large jelly onto a bed of apple purée. If serving the jelly in glasses, spoon a little apple purée over. Top with whole raspberries and serve.

sabayon of lady-finger bananas

with rum

Caramelised bananas are what French children learn to cook when on camping trips. The addition of rum and sabayon makes this more of an adult dish but, since almost all the alcohol evaporates during the cooking, children can enjoy it too.

SERVES 4

4 lady-finger bananas

3 tbsp caster sugar

2 egg yolks

1 tbsp orange juice

2 tsp finely grated orange zest

2 tbsp rum

50 g (almost 2 oz) butter

a little icing sugar for dusting

Cut the bananas diagonally in 2 cm (1 in) slices and sprinkle with 2½ tablespoons of the caster sugar.

Place the egg yolks in a largish metal bowl with the orange juice, zest, ½ tablespoon of the rum and the remaining caster sugar. Position the bowl over a saucepan of hot (not boiling) water with the bowl touching the water. Whisk the yolks vigorously until they are light and fluffy. (This takes around 10 minutes: if your arms get tired with all the whisking, take turns with someone else.) Remove the bowl from the saucepan.

Preheat the griller. Heat the butter in a large frying pan on top of the stove, add the bananas and cook until lightly caramelised and soft. Add the remaining rum, and boil for 1 minute. Arrange the banana slices in a large ovenproof dish or individual gratin dishes. Spoon the egg mixture over the bananas and dust with icing sugar. Place under the grill for 1 or 2 minutes, until the top is golden, and serve immediately.

frozen cappuccino soufflé

S E R V E S 4–6, D E P E N D I N G O N

S I Z E O F T H E C U P S

1 cup milk

¼ vanilla bean, split lengthwise

2 egg yolks

50 g (almost 2 oz) caster sugar

25 g (almost 1 oz) plain flour, sifted

1 tbsp instant coffee or 1 tsp coffee extract

1 cup cream

3 egg whites

a pinch of cream of tartar

50 g (almost 2 oz) icing sugar

a little cocoa and extra icing sugar for dusting

It is best to prepare this 4–6 hours before it's required. Use your most attractive small coffee cups, fitted with a double strip of baking paper to form a collar extending 3 cm (1½ in) above the rim.

Bring the milk and vanilla bean to the boil in a small saucepan. Meanwhile, whisk the egg yolks and caster sugar together in a bowl for about 2 minutes. Stir in the sifted flour until just combined, then pour in the hot milk and whisk until combined. Return this mixture to the saucepan and cook over a medium heat, still whisking constantly. When the mixture has thickened, transfer it to a bowl, whisk in the coffee and allow to cool. When the custard is cold, whip the cream and fold it in.

Beat the egg whites and cream of tartar until slightly stiff, then add the icing sugar and beat until stiff peaks form. Gently fold the beaten whites into the custard and spoon the mixture into the prepared cups, to a level of about 2 cm (¾ in) above the rim. Freeze until set.

Five minutes before serving, remove the soufflés from the freezer. Dust the top with cocoa and icing sugar, remove the paper collars and serve.

vanilla ice-cream

This is best made with an ice-cream machine. If you use fresh free-range eggs, full-cream milk and a quality vanilla bean, it is incomparable.

MAKES ABOUT 2 LITRES
(ABOUT 4 PTS)

10 egg yolks

300 g (about 11 oz) caster sugar

4 cups full-cream milk

1 vanilla bean

2 cups cream, whipped

Using an electric mixer, beat the egg yolks and caster sugar for 8–10 minutes until the mixture becomes lighter in colour and forms ribbons.

Pour the milk into a largish saucepan. Split the vanilla bean in half and scrape the tiny seeds into the milk. Add the bean to the milk and bring to the boil. Then, whisking all the time, slowly pour the hot milk over the beaten egg yolks and combine well.

Return the mixture to the pan and stir thoroughly over a medium heat with a wooden spatula, reaching all around the edges of the pan to stop the custard sticking. (Do not allow the custard to boil at any stage, or it will curdle.) The mixture will thicken slightly and, after a few minutes, lightly coat the spatula. Remove from the heat and strain into a bowl, stirring for a further 10 seconds, then leave to cool.

Gently mix the whipped cream into the cold custard and churn it in the ice-cream maker until set. Cover the ice-cream and store in a suitable container in the freezer. It keeps well for a week, but the fresher the better: you can halve the quantities if you wish.

CHOCOLATE ICE-CREAM
For a delicious chocolate variation, prepare the custard and strain it as described above. While it is still hot, add 150 g (about 5 oz) of dark cooking chocolate and stir well until it melts. Leave to cool, then add the whipped cream and churn and freeze the mixture.

Note: If you don't have an ice-cream maker, put the ice-cream preparation in a stainless-steel bowl and place it in the freezer. Allow it to set a little (this may take about 45 minutes) and then whisk it for about 10 seconds. Return it to the freezer to set a little more, then whisk again to give it extra lightness and to stop large ice crystals forming.

pear, kirsch and pistachio ice-cream

Serves 6–8

4 large pears (preferably Williams)

juice of 2 oranges

juice of $\frac{1}{2}$ lemon

1 tbsp Kirsch, Poire Williams liqueur, or brandy

about 1$\frac{1}{4}$ cups caster sugar

$\frac{1}{2}$ cup cream, whipped

50 g (almost 2 oz) raw pistachio nuts

For this you can use either very sweet ripe pears or poached pears. Or substitute fresh mangoes for the pears and almonds or hazelnuts for the pistachios.

Peel, quarter and core the pears. In a food processor, blend them to a purée with the orange juice, lemon juice, Kirsch and sugar. Mix the whipped cream into the pear purée, place in an ice-cream maker and churn until almost set. (If you don't have an ice-cream machine, see the note at the foot of page 154.)

Meanwhile, plunge the pistachios into boiling water for 10 seconds. Drain and skin them, then chop into small pieces. Add the nuts to the ice-cream when it is nearly firm, then churn again until set. Transfer the ice-cream to a special mould or container and store in the freezer until required.

strawberry or raspberry sorbet
with vanilla

500 g (about 1 lb) very sweet strawberries

or raspberries

juice of 2 oranges

juice of 1 lemon

1$\frac{1}{2}$ cups caster sugar

$\frac{1}{2}$ vanilla bean

Make this tantalising sorbet when the fruits are at their best—that is, when you smell their sweet fragrance as soon as you enter the greengrocer's shop. The ice is best eaten freshly made, but it keeps well (covered) in the freezer for 3–4 days.

Wash and hull the strawberries. If using raspberries, do not wash them. In a food processor, purée the berries with the orange and lemon juices and the sugar. (For a raspberry sorbet, strain the purée to eliminate the seeds.)

Split the vanilla bean in half lengthwise, scrape out the tiny seeds and mix these into the fruit purée. Pour the mixture into an ice-cream maker and churn until firm. (If you don't have an ice-cream machine, see the note at the foot of page 154.) Transfer to a pre-chilled mould, cover with plastic wrap and a lid, and store in the freezer.

marrons glacés and rum ice-cream

Mediterranean Europeans are very fond of candied chestnuts, which often appear at special occasions in the same way as champagne. This festive ice-cream, made with marinated chestnuts and rum-soaked sultanas, is ideal for an Australian Christmas.

SERVES 6–8

100 g (about 3½ oz) marrons glacés (they don't need to be whole)

50 g (almost 2 oz) sultanas

2 tbsp rum

6 egg yolks

150 g (about 5 oz) caster sugar

2 cups full-cream milk

½ vanilla bean, split lengthwise

1 cup whipped cream

Break the marrons glacés into small pieces the size of hazelnuts. Place in a bowl with the sultanas and the rum, and toss gently without breaking the marrons any further. Cover with plastic wrap or foil, and set aside.

Using an electric mixer, beat the egg yolks and caster sugar for 8–10 minutes until the mixture lightens in colour and forms ribbons.

Now bring the milk to the boil with the vanilla bean in a medium-sized saucepan. Whisking constantly, pour the hot milk over the beaten egg yolks, then return the mixture to the pan. Using a wooden spatula, stir thoroughly over a medium heat, reaching all around the edges of the pan to stop the custard sticking. (Do not allow it to boil, or it will curdle.) After a few minutes, when the mixture has thickened slightly and lightly coats the spatula, remove from the heat and strain into a bowl. Stir for a further 10 seconds, then leave to cool.

Gently mix the whipped cream into the cold custard, then churn this mixture in an ice-cream maker until almost set. (If you don't have an ice-cream machine, see the note at the foot of page 154.) Drain the rum from the bowl of chestnuts into the ice-cream and churn again until set. Transfer to an ice-cream container or mould, at the same time mixing in the chestnuts and sultanas. Cover and store in the freezer.

praliné and grand marnier ice-cream

I have a really soft spot for this ice-cream, which I made hundreds of times during my chef's apprenticeship in the Loire Valley. It's lovely served with a small slice of chocolate cake. (If serving it to young children, omit the Grand Marnier.)

SERVES 8

6 egg yolks (60 g eggs)
200 g (about 7 oz) caster sugar
2 cups full-cream milk
½ vanilla bean
½ tbsp instant coffee
2 tbsp cold water
2 drops red wine vinegar
100 g (about 3½ oz) roasted hazelnuts, preferably skinned
1 cup whipped cream
2 tbsp Grand Marnier

Using an electric mixer, beat the egg yolks and 150 g (about 5 oz) of the caster sugar on medium speed for 8–10 minutes until the mixture turns a lighter colour and forms ribbons.

Pour the milk into a medium-sized saucepan. Split the vanilla bean in half lengthwise and scrape the tiny seeds into the milk. Add the vanilla bean to the pan, bring the milk to the boil and then whisking slowly, pour it onto the beaten egg yolks and combine well. Return the mixture to the pan and stir thoroughly with a wooden spatula over a medium heat, reaching all around the edges of the pan to stop the custard sticking. (Do not allow the custard to boil at any stage, or it will curdle.) After a few minutes, the mixture will thicken and lightly coat the spatula. Remove from heat and strain into a bowl, stirring for a further 10 seconds. Stir in the instant coffee and leave to cool.

Put the cold water, vinegar and remaining sugar in a small stainless-steel pan and cook over a medium heat until it turns a golden caramel colour. Stir in the hazelnuts, using a wooden spoon, and cook for about 30 seconds until the nuts are coated with caramel. Pour them onto a lightly oiled piece of foil and leave to cool. When cold, blend or cut them into small pieces, reserving 12 whole ones for decoration.

When the custard is cold, gently mix in the whipped cream then churn the mixture in an ice-cream maker until almost set. (If you don't have an ice-cream machine, see the note at the foot of page 154.) Add the Grand Marnier and churn again until set. Add the chopped hazelnuts and mix well. Transfer the ice-cream to an attractive mould, cover with foil and place in the freezer.

To serve, unmould the ice-cream and top with the remaining whole caramelised hazelnuts.

hazelnut meringue and pear cake

A variation on the dacquoise (page 127). It is easiest to make a rectangular cake: for a round one you will need to cook three disks of meringue, each about 18 cm (about 7 in) in diameter.

SERVES 8

MERINGUE

60 g (about 2 oz) hazelnut meal

4 egg whites

a pinch of cream of tartar

180 g (about 6 oz) caster sugar

2 drops red wine vinegar

3 drops vanilla essence

1 tbsp cornflour

FILLING AND FINISHING

120 g (about 4 oz) plump dried pears

300 ml (about ½ pt) cream

1 tbsp sugar

120 g (about 4 oz) flaked almonds, browned

icing sugar for dusting the cake

Preheat the oven to 180°C/350°F.

Place the hazelnut meal in a dry pan and brown lightly over a medium heat. Transfer to a bowl and allow to cool.

Beat the egg whites with the cream of tartar until almost stiff. Gently beat in two-thirds of the sugar, the vinegar and the vanilla essence, continuing to beat at a low speed until the mixture forms stiff peaks.

Mix the remaining caster sugar with the cornflour and hazelnut meal, then fold this into the beaten egg whites. Pour this meringue mixture, spreading it evenly, onto a baking sheet 35 cm × 25 cm (14 in × 10 in) which you have lined with baking paper. Bake in the preheated oven for 25–30 minutes: the cooked meringue should be firm and dry. Remove from oven and allow to cool.

Now to fill and finish the cake. Remove any pips from the dried pears and place pears in a saucepan. Cover with cold water and boil for 10 minutes. Drain well and blend pears to a very fine purée. Allow to cool.

Whip the cream and mix in the sugar. Using a serrated knife, cut the meringue into three long, equal strips. Spread two of them with the pear purée, then with two-thirds of the whipped cream. Stack the layers, placing the ungarnished one on top, flat side up. Spread the sides with remaining cream.

Take a handful of flaked almonds and press them lightly onto the sides of the cake. Dust the top with icing sugar and place on a serving plate. Cut into 8 slices.

raspberry and vanilla soufflé

During my early years as a chef, soufflés were seen as the ultimate dessert, a light and exquisite way to finish a special meal. Even nowadays they are high on my list of favourites and I sometimes serve a soufflé instead of a cake for afternoon tea.

SERVES 6

1 quantity of crème patissière (page 176)

300 g (about 11 oz) raspberries

150 g (about 5 oz) caster sugar

½ vanilla bean, split lengthwise

6 tbsp cold water

a little butter and caster sugar to prepare the moulds

a pinch of cream of tartar

6 egg whites

1 tbsp Kirsch, cognac or brandy

icing sugar for dusting

Prepare the crème pâtissière and leave to cool.

Place the raspberries in a saucepan with 120 g (about 4 oz) of the caster sugar, the vanilla bean and the water. Boil for 5 minutes, then remove the vanilla bean. Blend everything to a purée, then pass it through a fine strainer. Transfer this sauce to a small saucepan and simmer for about 5 minutes or until it has the texture of thin jam.

Preheat oven to 200°C/400°F. Grease individual soufflé moulds with the butter and dust with sugar.

Add the cream of tartar to the egg whites and beat with an electric beater until firm. Add the remaining caster sugar and beat until the mixture forms stiff peaks.

Mix the raspberry sauce and Kirsch into the crème pâtissière. Stir in a small amount of the beaten egg whites, then gently fold in the remainder using a large metal spoon or rubber spatula. Fill the prepared moulds with this soufflé mixture and flatten the top with a spatula. Using a small piece of kitchen paper, carefully wipe any mixture from the rims of the moulds. Place moulds on an oven sheet, leaving a space between each, and bake in the preheated oven for about 12 minutes. When the soufflés have risen and are browned lightly on the top and sides, dust with icing sugar and place carefully on a plate. Serve immediately.

Although there are many fine food stores catering for all our needs, there is nothing better than making your own pastries, stocks and sauces. It gives you great satisfaction and the results are incomparable.

Pastries and stocks can be made up to three days in advance, or two months if you are freezing them. A good stock is an infusion of fresh bones (preferably free of fat and blood), plenty of aromatic vegetables such as celery, leeks, carrots and onions, some herbs (parsley, thyme and bayleaf for example) and spices. It is best if a stock simmers rather than boils, for this helps to keep it clear. The bigger the bones, the longer the stock will need to cook.

Making good pastries is one of the most satisfying achievements for a cook, in some ways akin to learning a craft such as pottery or drawing. And you certainly get better as you go along. Delicate pastries are best made in a cool kitchen. On hot days you may need to cool the flour and sugar slightly in the refrigerator before use. Avoid overmixing or overhandling dough pastry and once it is mixed, place it in the fridge to rest for about 30 minutes before rolling it out. Keep the bench and rolling-pin well floured while rolling the pastry.

beef or veal stock

MAKES 2 LITRES
(ABOUT 4 PTS)

2–3 kg (about 4–6 lb) veal or beef bones,
cut into 5 cm (2 in) pieces
1 large onion, quartered
2 tbsp vegetable oil
1 veal shank or oxtail
2 medium carrots, halved
2 sticks of celery, each cut into 3 pieces
1 clove
6 peppercorns, crushed
4 sprigs of parsley
1 bayleaf
2 sprigs of thyme
1 tsp sea salt
1 tsp tomato paste

Have fun and make an afternoon of it. Use your largest pot to make a rich stock that you can then freeze ready for use in special dishes when you want it.

Preheat the oven to 250°C/500°F.

Place the bones and onion in a large mixing bowl and toss with the oil. Transfer to a roasting tray and brown in the preheated oven for 15–25 minutes. Remove from the oven, drain off the fat and transfer the bones and onion to a stockpot. Add the veal shank or oxtail and the remaining ingredients, cover with cold water and bring to the boil. Reduce the heat and simmer for 3 hours, skimming the surface occasionally with a mesh spoon to remove any scum.

Strain the stock into a saucepan and boil down to reduce to about 8 cups, or less if you wish the stock to be strong. Allow to cool, then skim off any surface fat. Refrigerate for up to 4 days or freeze for up to 2 months.

chicken stock

Makes about 2 litres
(about 4 pts)

1 chicken or 1.5 kg (about 3 lb) chicken bones

3 litres (about 5½ pts) cold water

a few sprigs of parsley

2 sprigs of thyme

1 small bay leaf

2 medium-sized carrots, each cut into 3 pieces

1 onion, halved

2 sticks of celery or a small leek, cut into large chunks

1 tsp sea salt

8 black peppercorns, crushed

2 cloves

Rich and delicate, a flavoursome chicken stock adds body to soups, sauces, risottos and many other dishes. It can be refrigerated for a few days, or will keep in the freezer for about two months. At home when we make stock, we cook extra and freeze it for future use. In this recipe you can use a whole chicken, which then provides a meal, or just use chicken bones: the results are equally good and the choice is yours.

Place chicken or bones in a saucepan and cover with cold water. Bring to the boil and skim the surface to remove foam as it appears.

Tie the parsley, thyme and bay leaf together with kitchen string to make a bouquet garni. Add this to the pot with the carrots, onion, celery, salt, peppercorns and cloves. Simmer for about 50 minutes, skimming the surface, if necessary. Strain the stock and allow it to cool before storing in the fridge: it will keep there for 3–4 days. When cold, remove any fat from the surface. The stock will keep for 2 months in the freezer.

The poached chicken and vegetables make a delicious soup reheated in some of the stock. Or you can serve the chicken meat and the vegetables cold, with a dressing of olive oil, vinegar, chopped parsley and garlic.

fish stock

3 sprigs of parsley

1 sprig of thyme

½ bay leaf

1 medium-sized carrot

1 stick of celery

1 medium-sized brown onion

500 g (about 1 lb) cleaned sea-fish bones

20 g (about ⅔ oz) butter

⅓ cup dry white wine

water

salt

Fish stock has many uses. It can form the liquid for a soup, it can be used for seafood sauces or to poach fish. Ask your fishmonger for very clean bones (no gills, no guts) from sea fish such as snapper, John Dory or flathead: river fish does not make good fish stock.

Tie the parsley, thyme and bay leaf together with string. Wash the carrot and celery and slice thinly. Slice the onion. Chop the fish bones into 10 cm (4 in) pieces.

Put the butter in a large saucepan over a medium heat and gently stir-fry the vegetables for about 5 minutes. Add the herbs, fish bones and wine, cover with cold water and season with a little salt. Bring to the boil, simmer for 20 minutes and then strain through a fine strainer.

If you are not using the stock at once, you can reduce it by boiling it, for ease of storage. Allow it to cool and, when cold, remove any fat from the surface. Store in the fridge for 2–3 days, or in the freezer for 1–2 months.

prawn stock

When you peel green prawns and throw away the shells, lots of beautiful flavour is wasted. The shells can be transformed into a delicious stock suitable to use in a soup, sauce or risotto.

MAKES ABOUT 1 LITRE (ABOUT 2 PTS)

2 tbsp olive oil

2–3 cups prawn shells, including the heads

1/2 brown onion, chopped

1/4 cup dry white wine

about 5 cups cold water

3 sprigs of parsley

salt and freshly ground black pepper

Heat the oil in a saucepan and stir-fry the prawn shells over a high heat for 3–4 minutes. Add the onion and stir for a further minute. Add the wine, bring to the boil and add the water, parsley and a little salt and pepper. Return to the boil and simmer for 15 minutes.

Strain the stock, pressing on the prawn shells to extract as much flavour as possible.

vegetable stock

All vegetables have quite different aromatic flavours. When you cook a few together in a liquid, you obtain a delicious broth that can be used as a soup or stock. It is particularly good for vegetarians.

MAKES ABOUT 2 LITRES
(ABOUT 4 PTS)

1/2 tbsp olive oil

1 brown onion, sliced

2 carrots, sliced

2 sticks of celery, sliced

1 small leek, washed and sliced

12 cups cold water

2 sprigs of thyme

4 sprigs of parsley

1 clove

salt and freshly ground black pepper

Heat the oil in a non-stick saucepan and stir-fry the onion until lightly browned. Add the carrot, celery and leek, and stir-fry for about 3 minutes. Add the water, thyme, parsley and clove, and season with salt and pepper. Simmer, uncovered, for about 20 minutes.

Strain the broth and allow it to cool before storing. If you wish, you can make a purée with the vegetables: just remove the herbs first, and add a small knob of butter.

THE GOOD

oil

ANY FOOD THAT HAS BEEN CULTIVATED FOR SIX THOUSAND YEARS MUST be good. This is certainly true of the olive, in terms of both our health and its flavour. The olive is a native to the countries bordering the Mediterranean, where it is still mainly grown: Spain, Italy, Greece, Turkey, Tunisia and Portugal are the largest producers. It also does well in other regions with a dry Mediterranean-style climate, including China, South America, the United States, Australia and South Africa. The olive tree is not particularly fussy about the soil in which it grows. In fact, poor, chalky soils often produce high-quality olives. There are more than 750 million olive trees in the world, which produce about thirty different varieties of fruit. Most of the world's olive crop is grown for oil.

The olives are harvested in winter and collected in large nets spread under the tree, and much care is taken not to damage them. They are then transported to the mill, where they are classified according to quality, washed and then crushed to a paste, pits and all. As the fruit deteriorate rapidly, crushing takes place as soon as possible after picking. The olive paste is pressed gently to extract the oil, which is then filtered and stored ready for consumption.

Olive oil is best consumed within a few months of manufacture. When cooking with olive oil, it is interesting to experiment with oils from different regions. In salads and seasonings, and some dishes where the flavour of the oil is important, I use a good-quality extra-virgin olive oil. For other purposes I use a more affordable variety.

sweet pastry

MAKES TWO 25 CM (10 IN) ROUND TARTS OR 20 SMALL INDIVIDUAL TARTS

60 g (about 2 oz) almonds, chopped small
150 g (about 5 oz) unsalted butter, cut in small cubes
1 large egg
1 tsp finely grated lemon zest or
¼ tsp vanilla essence
a pinch of salt
100 g (about 3½ oz) icing sugar
250 g (about 9 oz) plain flour

A superb pastry which is easy to work with. It is best made a few hours or the day before you need it, so it can rest. Cut the almonds into pieces a little smaller than peppercorns.

Place the almonds, butter, egg, lemon zest and salt in a food mixer and blend until just combined. Gradually add the icing sugar and flour, and mix again until just combined. Form the pastry into a ball, but don't overwork or overheat it. Wrap in plastic wrap or foil, flatten slightly and leave to rest in the fridge for at least 1 hour before using.

If you don't have a mixer, place the flour in a bowl. Make a well in the centre and put into it the egg, butter, lemon zest, salt and sugar. Mix these ingredients first, using your fingertips, then incorporate the flour with the whole hand, until just combined. Form the pastry into a ball, flatten slightly, wrap in plastic wrap or foil, and leave in the fridge for at least 1 hour before using.

puff pastry

There are various steps and resting times involved, so this takes about two hours to make. Plan ahead and make it the day before you need it (or you can freeze it).

MAKES 1.2 KG
(ABOUT 2¼ LB) OF PASTRY

1 tsp salt

400 g (about 14 oz) unsalted butter

500 g (about 1 lb) plain flour

1 cup cold water

In a mixer, beat the salt and 125 g (about 4 oz) of the butter until soft. Slowly add the flour and water and beat until well incorporated. Form the pastry into a ball, wrap in plastic wrap and refrigerate for 30 minutes. (If you don't have an electric mixer, use a food processor or a hand-beater.)

Cut the remaining butter into 1 cm (½ in) slices. Remove the pastry from the fridge and roll it out to a square about 1 cm (½ in) thick. Place the butter slices in the centre and fold the four edges inwards to cover the butter.

STEP 1

Roll out the pastry to a rectangular strip 1 cm (½ in) thick and about twice as long as it is wide. Fold the bottom end of the strip up a third of the way toward the top. Fold the top end down to fit over the first fold, forming a neat rectangle with no overlapping sides.

STEP 2

Shift the pastry a quarter turn to the right. Again roll it out to a strip 1 cm (½ in) thick and fold it exactly as before. Make a small impression with your fingertip in the top right-hand corner of the pastry.

STEP 3

Wrap the pastry in plastic wrap and refrigerate for 20 minutes to allow the butter and pastry to combine well.

Remove the pastry from the fridge and place it on the table with your fingertip mark in the bottom right-hand corner. Now repeat steps 1, 2 and 3.

Remove the pastry from the fridge and repeat steps 1 and 2. This time there is no need to make a finger mark because the pastry is completed and ready to use. It is wise, however, to chill it slightly before use, so it is easier to roll out.

crème anglaise (custard sauce)

Makes 2½–3 cups (8–10 serves)

5 egg yolks (size 61 g eggs)
150 g (about 5 oz) caster sugar
2 cups milk
⅓ vanilla pod, split lengthwise

A delicious accompaniment for puddings, cakes and fruits, this classic custard sauce is also an important ingredient in a bavarois. For something a little richer, add some whipped cream to the cold custard just before serving.

In a medium-sized mixing bowl, beat the egg yolks and sugar for 8–10 minutes or until the mixture forms ribbons. Bring the milk and vanilla to the boil in a 2 litre saucepan. Pour slowly onto the egg mixture and whisk well. Return to the pan and, using a wooden spatula, stir over a medium heat until the custard thickens slightly and lightly coats the back of the spatula. (Do not allow the custard to boil, or the eggs will curdle.) Remove from heat, strain into a bowl and whisk for a few seconds more (discard the vanilla pod). If the custard begins to separate or scramble, whisk in 2 tablespoons of cold milk to stop it cooking any further. Cover and refrigerate when cold.

crème pâtissière (french custard cream)

Makes about 3 cups

2 cups milk
⅓ vanilla pod, split lengthwise
4 egg yolks
100 g (about 4 oz) caster sugar
50 g (almost 2 oz) plain flour, sifted

This popular French custard is used to garnish fruit tarts and choux pastries. It also forms the base for many soufflés.

In a largish saucepan, bring the milk to the boil with the vanilla pod. Meanwhile, whisk the egg yolks and caster sugar in a medium-sized bowl for about 4 minutes. Stir in the sifted flour, but don't overmix.

Pour the hot milk slowly onto the flour and egg mixture, whisking well. Return the mixture to the pan and cook over a low heat for a few minutes, still whisking constantly, until it thickens. Transfer to a bowl and whisk the custard for a few seconds until smooth. Allow to cool before covering with plastic wrap and refrigerating: it will keep for 2–3 days.

conversions

VOLUME

1 metric teaspoon	=	1 US teaspoon
	=	5 ml
½ metric tablespoon	=	10 ml
1 metric tablespoon	=	20 ml
½ US tablespoon	=	7.5 ml
1 US tablespoon	–	15 ml
¼ metric cup	=	62.5 ml
	=	a little over 2 oz
½ metric cup	=	125 ml
	=	about 4½ oz
1 metric cup	=	250 ml
	=	about 9 oz
4 metric cups	=	1000 ml
	=	about 36 oz

MEASURES

3 mm	=	⅛ in		
5 mm	=	½ cm	=	⅕ in
1 cm	=	⅓ in		
2 cm	=	⅔ in		
2.5 cm	=	1 in		
5 cm	=	2 in		

OVEN TEMPERATURES

100°C = 210°F
VERY SLOW
(just to reheat)

125°C = 240°F
VERY SLOW

150°C – 300°F
SLOW:
Thermostat 1 for large cakes, roasts and casseroles

180°C = 350°F
MODERATE:
Thermostat 4 for cakes and roasts

200°C = 400°F
MODERATELY HOT:
Thermostat 6 for gratins and small roasts

220°C = 450°F
HOT:
Thermostat 7 to brown food quickly

250°C = 500°F
VERY HOT:
Thermostat 9 for breads and pizzas

WEIGHT

15 g	=	½ oz
30 g	=	1 oz
60 g	=	2 oz
90 g	=	3 oz
100 g	=	3½ oz
150 g	=	5 oz
200 g	=	7 oz
250 g	=	9 oz
500 g	=	about 1 lb

APPROXIMATE CUP EQUIVALENTS VOLUME FOR WEIGHT

1 cup flour	=	175 g
1 cup rice	=	220 g
1 cup sugar	=	240 g
1 cup water	=	250 g